Inspiring | Educating | Creating | Entertaining

Brimming with creative inspiration, how-to projects, and useful
information to enrich your everyday life, Quarto Knows is a favorite
destination for those pursuing their interests and passions. Visit our
site and dig deeper with our books into your area of interest:
Quarto Creates, Quarto Cooks, Quarto Homes, Quarto Lives,
Quarto Drives, Quarto Explores, Quarto Gifts, or Quarto Kids.

This book provides general information on various widely known and widely accepted images that tend
to evoke feelings of strength and confidence. However, it should not be relied upon as recommending or
promoting any specific diagnosis or method of treatment for a particular condition, and it is not intended
as a substitute for medical advice or for direct diagnosis and treatment of a medical condition by a
qualified physician. Readers who have questions about a particular condition, possible treatments for that
condition, or possible reactions from the condition or its treatment should consult a physician or other
qualified healthcare professional.

IN FOCUS

Reiki

Your Personal Guide

DES HYNES

WELLFLEET
PRESS

CONTENTS

AN INTRODUCTION TO REIKI

Holistic healing involves treating the mind, body, and soul as one entity rather than treating the symptoms alone, and Reiki, in its different forms, is at the center of many holistic healing practices. In this book, we will look at some causes of illness along with ways in which we can aid the healing process for ourselves and others by using the connection between the mind, body, and soul. We will also see how cases that would have been described as miracles in the past are becoming more accepted as the results of holistic healing methods such as Reiki, which themselves are becoming more and more popular, perhaps due in part to the rising costs of health care.

If You Get Sick

If you get sick or have an accident, you must consult an appropriate doctor, surgeon, hospital, or specialist and allow that medical professional to treat the problem by conventional means. Please keep in mind that the information and techniques in this book do not constitute medical advice and it is not intended to replace such advice. The author and publishers cannot accept responsibility for any illness that occurs as a result of the reader not seeking medical advice from a qualified doctor. Above all, please use common sense.

My First Encounter with Reiki

Ten years ago, I had never even heard of Reiki. I first came across it while my wife, Viv, was being treated for cancer. As you may know, the side effects of chemotherapy can be horrendous, which is not surprising considering that chemotherapy was developed from mustard gas, which was used extensively for chemical warfare during the First World War!

The hospital that was treating Viv offered Reiki to help combat the side effects of the chemotherapy, a common practice in many major hospitals in England, and I soon started to notice that after each Reiki session Viv was

THE ORIGINS OF CHEMOTHERAPY

◆

Mustard gas was used again during World War II, when naval personnel were exposed to the gas during a Luftwaffe raid on allied ships in the naval base in Bari, Italy. Hundreds of sailors jumped into the water to escape from the sinking ships and when they emerged, they were covered with an oily substance that had leaked from the damaged ships. Many noticed a garlicky odor in the air and complained of a burning sensation on their skin. At first, they thought it must be the engine oil, but then blisters began to form. Among the twenty-eight destroyed ships was the SS *John Harvey* with a cargo that contained 120,000 pounds of mustard gas that had leaked into the harbor. It was only while testing tissue samples from the victims that doctors noticed the depletion of white blood cells, and it was from this that researchers developed nitrogen mustard, which proved therapeutic for people with leukemia and lymphoma—cancers that originate in white blood cells. From this, other chemicals were developed to target different types of cancer cells.

calmer and less stressed. She also felt better within herself. Viv fought against the cancer for four years and while she did succumb to it in the end, the Reiki healing that she been given made her life, and her death, much easier than it might otherwise have been.

The Benefits of a Holistic Approach

I believe that medication should be used to assist the body to heal itself and not as a long-term solution, and it should be part of a holistic approach that treats the cause of the illness in the body, mind, and soul. The good news is that more and more people are looking to combine Western medicine with healing practices such as Reiki that aim to treat the whole of a person.

In ancient China, the village doctor got paid to prevent illness, so if nobody got ill he was doing his job well, but if too many people got sick, he was fired!

When we are ill we lose our appetite, which is a message from our bodies telling us to give our digestive system a chance to rest. Our bodies use energy to turn the food we eat into fuel to sustain life, but this energy can be redirected to help with our natural healing ability. Each one of us is equipped with amazing and sophisticated healing processes that make our bodies repair and maintain themselves—as long as we allow them to do so.

It is believed that the liver gradually replaces itself every few months, the skin is renewed every month, and the stomach lining every four days. Many things influence this natural regeneration. We need to eat a healthy, balanced diet and drink plenty of water. Keeping stress to a minimum, taking some exercise, and getting sufficient sleep are also important for maintaining health, while overcoming a serious illness demands even more from us. Reiki is a powerful means of helping us to attain good health by a holistic approach.

What Is Reiki?

Reiki is a Japanese technique for stress reduction and relaxation that also promotes healing through using the energy of a higher, divine, guided life force. The word *Reiki* is used both for the name of the practice and for the healing energy involved. Reiki is noninvasive, and it doesn't require a person to remove their clothes to be treated, although people do typically take off their glasses and shoes before a treatment, to make themselves comfortable.

If you are interested in becoming a Reiki healer, you must be aware that Reiki can change your life. With regular Reiki treatments, you will be less stressed and more compassionate—a different person. Since discovering Reiki, I rarely drink alcohol and I became a vegetarian, which are elements of a gradual change that took many years. Engaging in Reiki also helped me to become aware of my spiritual path.

A healer doesn't have to guide the healing energy he produces, because once he starts the healing process and feels the energy flow, he only needs to remember these five words:

"Get out of the way."

- The Reiki healer must back off and allow the energy to flow through him to the person who needs it.
- Reiki can be used on its own or alongside conventional medicine to assist recovery.
- Reiki is not a religion based on belief or faith. All that is required is love and compassion.
- The energy generated is guided by a higher power, so the Reiki knows where to go and how to act on its own and because of this, Reiki can do no harm.

How Does Reiki Heal?

Reiki is a holistic form of energy healing. By holistic, we mean that it works on the mind, body, and spirit at the same time and success depends on a combination of conditions, such as the skill of the healer and the openness of the person receiving the healing. Reiki heals by balancing the body's energy centers and removing blockages. We healers are the link between the universal, divine energy and the higher self of the person we are working with. It is this higher self that accepts the healing, and because we all have free will, that person may or may not accept the healing.

Where Does the Healing Energy Come From?

Nothing is solid. Quantum physics says that 99.9999 percent of what is called matter is empty space. Within this space is energy and there is energy in everything from the smallest atom in our body to the sun that shines in the sky. Though we may not be able to see it, we know that it exists. We cannot see the wind, but we can feel and see its effect on the world around us. This universal energy exists in three heavens.

The first heaven is where we as humans live, and it is everything that we are aware of in our everyday lives. It is the physical Earth—the sea, mountains, and forests as well as everyone and everything that lives there. It is a combination of good and bad with a combination of healthy and unhealthy energies. There are people who want to help and those who want to take advantage. Each one of us has a bit of both good and bad to various degrees.

The second heaven is a psychic field of consciousness that is devoid of physical existence. This is where spirits who have passed over learn what they need for their further spiritual development. They can assist us here in the physical world, but just because they are on the other side of the veil does not mean that they are all-knowing. They still have an ego, so they may have  their own reasons to help us. They may use our own egos to impress us, making us think we are special. It is important when working with these guides that we remain in control. There are also spirits with highly refined energies within the second heaven. Remember these spirits are guides and as such they are only there to guide; it is we who must decide whether to allow them to help or not.

The third heaven is where divine healing energy comes from. We can all access the energy from the third heaven to varying degrees. For example, Jesus used the power of the Holy Spirit from the third heaven to heal and attune his disciples, thus allowing them to heal others in turn. There is no ego in the third heaven, only love and compassion. The energy in the third heaven comes from the divine source, and it is superior to all other forms of healing energies. We can connect directly with the third heaven from the first heaven, bypassing the second heaven. The heavenly beings in the third heaven will always respect our free will, so when we give healing with this divine energy, the person receiving the healing must also be willing to be healed.

Is Reiki Real?

My friend Roberta is a spiritual healer but she is *not* a Reiki healer. When Reiki first started to become known in the UK, Roberta was somewhat disturbed by its claims. It seemed that all Reiki healers needed to do was put their hands on their clients, while their minds were free to wander off somewhere else—planning their next vacation perhaps—and they had the *temerity* to call that *healing*? It made spiritual healing look like very hard work in comparison.

Roberta strongly suspected that Reiki wasn't real, and this notion was reinforced by the astonishing cost of training in those early days, which was about the price of a new car! It smacked of a con.

It was only later, when she was helping a friend write a book on Reiki and talking with other Reiki healers who were prepared to share a few secrets, that

she began to understand that a Reiki Master's training and initiation enable him or her to bring the Reiki in without expending the effort required for other forms of energy healing.

The History of Reiki

Reiki is an oral tradition that involves the transmission of energy from the teacher, usually called a Master, to the student during an initiation known as *attunement*. Each Reiki master has a Reiki lineage of this oral tradition that can be traced back to the system's founder, Dr. Mikao Usui (1865–1926), though the origins of the practice go back much deeper into history. Because of this lineage, Reiki is in many ways the same today as when the founder of the system was alive and practicing it.

Dr. Usui rediscovered Reiki in the early 1890s. It is said that he was teaching in a Christian seminary in Japan when one of his students asked him if he believed in the Bible stories about the healing that Jesus did, and, if so, when was he going to teach healing to the students?

It was then that Dr. Usui started his search for healing in both Buddhist and Christian texts. There is no real proof that Dr. Usui was in fact a Christian, but he may have embraced certain aspects of Christianity, such as love and compassion, in his search for spiritual advancement. It could also be that the Christian slant was given to Reiki to make it more appealing to Westerners. There are other influences that are said to be included in the foundation of Usui's Reiki, such as Tendai Buddhism (known as Mikkyo), Shintoism, and ideas from the world of martial arts and Shugendo, which is a path to mystic powers resulting from ascetic practices in the Japanese culture—a primitive type of mountain worship.

Dr. Usui did go to a sacred place called Mount Kurama, where he fasted and meditated. After twenty-one days he had a *satori*, which is the Japanese word traditionally meaning "one who has a fleeting glimpse or understanding of a higher order." During his satori Dr. Usui is believed to have been shown a series of symbols, written in the sky in gold, each with an accompanying mantra. It can therefore be said that Dr. Usui *rediscovered* Reiki because it had always been there.

The word *Reiki* (pronounced "Ray Kee") consists of two Japanese words: The first, *Rei*, means "universal" or "divine," and it is all-knowing. The second part, *Ki*, means "energy," which is the same word as *Chi* in China and *Prana* in India. So when we put it together, we have universal, or divine, energy.

Before Dr. Usui died in 1926, he taught several people his method of Reiki healing and made them Reiki Masters, or Reiki teachers. Mr. Chujiro Hayashi, a retired naval officer and surgeon in the Imperial Japanese Navy, took over from Dr. Usui after his death, inheriting the title of Reiki Grand Master.

Using his background as a surgeon, Mr. Hayashi used his technical knowledge of the way the human body works in order to create a Reiki student manual that listed illnesses and the various human organs. He also standardized the Reiki hand positions for healing. In the 1930s, Hayashi opened a healing clinic called the *Hayashi Reiki Kenkyu Kai* (Hayashi Spiritual Energy Research Society). It was run on a commercial basis, where people paid for their healing. Paying to receive Reiki is a way of showing respect for Reiki, and it was believed that if it was free, people would not value it; thus the healing became a form of exchange. On a personal note, I charge for the Reiki that I give, but I never charge those who are being treated for cancer. They usually bring me tea and biscuits, the latter of which is British English for cookies, of course!

By the year 1938, Hayashi had instructed thirteen Reiki Masters. In 1935, Hayashi met Ms. Hawayo Takata, an American-born Japanese woman who was part of a large Japanese community living in Hawaii at that time. Takata had gone to Japan to receive medical treatment, and after hearing about Hayashi's clinic, she hoped to recover from her illness without needing an operation. She did indeed regain her health without surgery, and she was so impressed that she became one of Hayashi's students. In 1938, Hayashi visited Hawaii and authorized Takata to teach Reiki, which she did, not only in Hawaii, but in the continental United States, and from there it spread around the world.

Just before he died in 1941, Hayashi declared Takata to be the Grand Master and head of the Reiki movement. Ms. Takata initiated only twenty-two Reiki Masters, so it was only after her death in 1980 that the Reiki movement expanded into various forms, which may also be due in part to the larger New Age movement.

The Spiritual Origins of Reiki

Since Dr. Usui rediscovered Reiki in the early part of the twentieth century, it has seen many transformations, but the Western style that many people practice today still uses the solid framework of what is now called *Usui Reiki*. It is as if someone bought an old house and installed new siding, central heating, modern plumbing, and a conservatory. On the outside it may look different, but the structure beneath is still the same. Some people believe that Reiki can be practiced without training and is seen as a gift. To a certain extent this is true, but with training come discipline and focus.

Before I accept someone who wants to learn Reiki as a student, I interview him to ascertain his suitability to be a Reiki practitioner. Some just see it as a business opportunity, a fast way to get people in and out the door with money pouring in as they do so. Reiki may take time to learn, but it is worth remembering that spiritual healers require two years of training before they can heal on their own.

The initial teaching of Usui Reiki is spiritual in nature. When we say *spiritual*, it is important to understand the difference between religious and spiritual practices. Religion normally has a dogma of principles that are believed to be undeniably true, infallible, and accepted without question. There may be manuscripts to support these beliefs. In Christianity this is the Bible, in Islam it is the Holy Koran, Hinduism uses the Vedas, Buddhism has the

Tripitaka, and in Judaism there are the Old Testament and the book of law, called the Talmud. Religions also normally have a priesthood and a central deity (God).

A spiritual practice, on the other hand, has none of these. Instead, it is an awareness gained through meditation and self-realization that leads to enlightenment. Dr. Usui taught his students how to connect with their own spirituality. The original attunement was a spiritual blessing given to the student. It was not to attune or empower someone, as the attunement is done today.

Dr. Usui came from a wealthy Buddhist family, and his parents encouraged him to study. He was both academically and physically talented, a practitioner of *Chi Kung*, also known as *Qi Gong*, which means "Life Energy Cultivation" and is a form of coordinated body posture and movement, breathing, and meditation to promote health, spirituality, and martial arts training. He was proficient in Samurai swordsmanship. Dr. Usui was also a member of *Rei Jyutu Ka*, a metaphysical group dedicated to developing psychic abilities.

At an early age, Dr. Usui became interested in medicine, the movement of energy in the body, and religion. He was searching for a way to heal with energy without depleting his own energy levels. During his quest, he traveled to China and the West. On his return to Japan, he undertook many different types of work, and eventually he was led back to his Buddhist roots to become a Tendai Buddhist monk. He moved to a monastery near Mount Kurama (Horse Saddle Mountain), where he continued his studies.

Tendai Buddhism came to Japan from China; it is a syncretistic movement, embracing other Buddhist schools from Vinaya to Zen, as well as Shinto, the indigenous Japanese tradition. Its distinct focus continued to be the teaching of Lotus Sutra, which is known for providing the means for salvation. It was during his time at the monastery that Dr. Usui enrolled in Isyu Guo, a 21-day training course to seek enlightenment that involved living in a cave, meditating, fasting, and praying. It was on the morning of the last day of the retreat that the Reiki energy entered Dr. Usui's crown chakra and he received the gift of Reiki.

Dr. Usui left the temple and dedicated the rest of his life to spreading the gift of Reiki healing. He opened a healing center, and it is said that for a brief period he worked in the slums, healing beggars in the Christian tradition. He is also supposed to have healed the victims of the Kanto earthquake that devastated Tokyo in 1923. On March 9, 1926, he died from a stroke. He is buried at the Saihoji temple, a Buddhist temple in the suburbs of Tokyo; it is also the resting place of his wife and son.

Saihoji Temple

Enclosed Meditation Cards

Included in this book are seven guided meditation cards based on the five Reiki principles, which you can find in chapter 7 (see pages 66–71). You can use them to relax, refocus, and re-center at any time and any place.

1

COMMON CAUSES
OF ILLNESS

We become sick when there is an imbalance in our physical or mental state. The cause of this imbalance may be environmental, psychological, or a combination of these. Most books on Reiki focus on the healing, but I believe that knowing the cause of the illness is just as important as the cure.

The places in which we live and work can influence our health. It is obvious that the air in the country or by the sea is healthier than the air quality in the city. It is not only the exhaust fumes from the traffic that are a problem in the city, but the "electronic smog" from a concentrated amount of electrical equipment may also be troublesome. When I was a child, the only electronic equipment in the house was the radio, or the *wireless* as it was known. Today most homes are packed with devices, and there will be many more in the future. Now even our vehicles are full of electronic equipment, and in cities, this abundance of technology is incredibly concentrated.

Having said that, considered medical investigation has shown that smoking, alcoholism, and obesity also contribute to the prevalence of cancer and many other serious health conditions.

I believe health comes down to an individual's immune system, which means that some people have better resistance to illness, while others are more vulnerable. It is a good idea to allow yourself some "me time" so that you can relax, and if you live in a city, be sure to get away from time to time and spend a day in the countryside or at the beach where you can breathe fresh, unpolluted air. Exercise is also important for building up resistance to illness.

The Psychological Causes of Illness

One of the biggest contributors to bad health is stress. What causes stress? Two of the main sources are anger and worry.

Anger + Worry = Stress = Illness

Anger

As part of the Reiki practitioner's code, there are five principles that we recite at least once a day, normally first thing in the morning. One of these principles is "Just for today, I will let go of anger." Notice that we say "Just for today." We are only promising ourselves that we will let go of anger today, because there are two days that we have no control over—yesterday and tomorrow—but the here and now is real.

We can get angry when people or things don't meet our expectations. Sometimes we get angry with ourselves if we don't meet the standards we set ourselves, and it is also common for us to get angry with those we care about the most. Anger is a very destructive emotion that can create serious blockages in one's energy field. It is the most complex inner enemy. We mistakenly think of being angry as giving us power over others, but the reverse is true, because anger clouds our judgment and makes us weak. Anger is a conscious choice, a habitual response, so everyone responds differently to similar situations.

I once treated a man whose hands shook uncontrollably, and the condition was getting worse. He'd had all the tests and his doctor could find no medical reason why this should have started, so as a last resort he came to me for a Reiki session. During the healing I noticed a blockage in his solar plexus chakra, so at the end of the treatment, I asked him if he was worried or got angry often, and he confirmed that he was under medication for anger issues.

To me, the best way to break a habitual response of anger is by practicing meditation and receiving Reiki healing. An angry person should also spend some time in nature, as a walk in the woods or a stroll along the beach helps him reconnect with the energy of nature that is so important for well-being.

Some will say, "My life is so busy that I never have time to do these things." It is up to all of us to make time. If we don't make time now, there may be plenty of time to reflect on where we went wrong when we are in the hospital.

Worry

Another Reiki principle is "Just for today I will let go of worry." While anger is about events that are happening or that have already happened, worry deals with future ones. Although worry is not always a negative phenomenon, endless worrying can take over one's thoughts, while each worry bores a small hole in the body and soul. And for what? Can you even remember what you were worried about this time last year or five years ago?

Listen

Try listening to meditation music during the evening when everyone else is watching television.

Worry is the fear of w*hat if.* What if I lose my Job? What if I get ill? What if the car breaks down? What if the roof leaks?

Worry can be emotional rather than practical: What if I marry the wrong person? What if my partner isn't being true to me? What if my partner doesn't really love me and approve of me? Worrying will not change an outcome, and nine out of ten things that we worry about never happen, so it is merely a habit that we get into, and like any bad habit, we can get rid of it.

We worry about our loved ones, but worrying about the problems of others is a waste of our time and energy. We can advise and support people, but we must accept that each one of us is a free spirit, and we all have the free will to choose for ourselves.

Stress

Everything that puts pressure on us causes stress. To some extent, stress is an inevitable part of being alive, and in many cases it has a positive purpose, in that it encourages us to make an effort rather than just lie around doing nothing. Depending on our personality type, the stress inherent in work or in working toward a  goal is useful, beneficial, and even enjoyable. However, there can be too much emphasis on deadlines, and if a person then has to come home to an unloving and difficult family, life becomes miserable. Eventually, this kind of stress piles up in the body and makes a person ill.

It is best to know yourself and avoid unnecessary pressure and stress where possible. When you are stressed, as we all are sometimes, Reiki healing can help you relax and bring down the level of tension that you are carrying around in your body.

❋ ❋ ❋

2

THE FIRST STEPS TO BECOMING A REIKI HEALER

Why Do You Want to Become a Reiki Healer?

This is a question I have asked many Reiki students, and two answers stand out. The first came from a middle-aged man named Ben. He had got my details from the UK Reiki Federation and told me he wanted to learn Reiki so that he could give healing to his dog, because it was getting old and suffering from arthritis. Ben had no desire to be a Reiki practitioner; he only wanted to ease the suffering of his dog.

On another occasion two girls came to me, and when I asked them why they wanted to learn Reiki, they said that they were hairdressers who worked in a beauty salon. Their boss had come up with the idea so that she could offer Reiki as an extra service to the clientele.

These stories demonstrate the two extremes: Ben wanted to be a healer to help a pet he loved, while the girls' boss was interested only in money. If the boss herself had wanted to be a Reiki healer, I would not have minded, but I thought that it disrespected Reiki to see it as just another form of beauty treatment.

The Need for a Teacher

There are healing methods that are physical in nature, such as reflexology, aromatherapy, and acupuncture, but when it comes to energy healing, it is hard for someone who is new to the idea to learn to channel and control the healing energies without help. Where Reiki is concerned, students really *do* need a teacher to guide them and show them what is real and what is not.

Reiki has four levels:

- Level one takes students to a point where they can give *themselves* Reiki healing.
- Level two is the one most people aim for, as it takes students to a stage where they can give Reiki to *others*, even on a professional basis.
- Level three takes students further and it introduces them to additional methods that they can adapt to work alongside the Reiki energy.
- Level four enables students to become Reiki Masters, which enables them to *teach* others.

There are special attunements (initiations) that can be carried out only by a Reiki Master, and at each level there are secrets that students learn, but these are of no use unless allied to proper attunements given by a Reiki Master. So even with the information that is now freely available on the internet, you still need to train in a hands-on manner if you are to become a Reiki healer.

NOTHING HAPPENS BY CHANCE

At this present moment in our lives we are where we are meant to be—which is not to say that this is where we *want* to be. Like actors in a play, there are others who have been instrumental in our present situation, but we also have free will, and we can always carry on with what we're doing or stop to consider making a change. Don't ever be afraid of making the wrong decisions—mistakes are all part of the learning process—but if you keep making the same mistake repeatedly, you need help to see what you are doing wrong. We all have guides whom we can ask for help while we are on our spiritual journey, and if we don't arrive at the desired location in this lifetime, we can pick up where we left off in the next incarnation.

We all have the ability to be healers because love and compassion reside in the divine spark within all our souls. Most people who become Reiki healers have themselves received Reiki, or they know someone who has had Reiki healing, so they have seen the benefits. Over the years I have taught and attuned many Reiki students, and I've noticed that there are certain types of people who are drawn to become Reiki healers. They are normally compassionate and caring people who have a strong desire to help others.

Finding a Teacher

Reiki is taught in the oral tradition with much of the knowledge passed down from Master to student, so it cannot be learned from books alone. There are many Reiki Masters out there, so it is important to find the one that you are drawn to. The International Center for Reiki Training and the UK Reiki Federation have lists of Reiki teachers all around the world, and all of these Reiki Masters and healers have a "Reiki lineage" that they can trace back to Reiki's founder, Mikao Usui. A person who teaches Reiki will not be offended if you ask to see their Reiki lineage.

It might also be beneficial to receive a Reiki treatment yourself so that you can experience the healing energy of Reiki on a personal basis prior to becoming a Reiki healer. You do not need to be ill to receive Reiki healing; for instance, I have a client who is an active elderly lady who comes to me on a monthly basis, purely to have her energy level topped up.

The Code of Ethics

Early in your Reiki journey, you will be given a Code of Ethics to read, and you will be asked to abide by this. Indeed, you may be asked to sign a copy of such a Code.

Degrees of Reiki

The four levels of Reiki, known as degrees, serve different purposes and have their own classes, attunements, and focuses.

First Degree: Shoden

The first degree centers on personal development, removing blockages you might have, and learning about the history of Reiki. You will also receive an attunement, hear about the twenty-one-day cleansing period, and discover how to give yourself a Reiki shower. This is also known as "byosen scanning," and it involves using the palm of the hand to detect imbalances in the body and chakras, weaknesses in the aura, and areas of the body that aren't functioning as they should.

Tip

You will not be shown the Reiki symbols during this level.

Second Degree: Okuden

Once you have completed level one, you can stay where we are and use your Reiki on yourself or your family, friends, pets, and plants, but many want to move to the next level so they can widen the circle of people they can help and maybe even become a professional Reiki practitioner. There is normally a gap of at least three months between level one and level two.

Third Degree: Junshihan

The third degree is the advanced training for a potential Reiki Master practitioner. It is normally a one-day training course, during which you will receive the Usui Master symbol and the Usui Master attunement. This will increase the strength of your Reiki energy, and you will also then be able to use the Master symbol in healing.

Tip

In the third degree, you will learn how to charge crystals with Reiki and how to make a Reiki grid using crystals. You will also learn how to perform aura healing, also called psychic surgery, which allows you to remove negative psychic energy from your clients and send the energy to the light.

Fourth Degree: Shihan

This is the three-day Master/Teacher course for advanced Reiki training. This is an intensive course that covers all you have learned in your previous training courses and teaches you ways of giving Reiki attunements for all levels of Reiki. You will also receive the Reiki training manuals that cover your courses.

Tip

If you are taking a Holy Fire course, you will also learn the Holy Fire symbol and receive the Holy Fire ignitions and Holy Fire meditations.

3

SHODEN: THE FIRST DEGREE OF REIKI STUDY

There are set syllabuses for each of the degrees of Reiki study, so there is a uniformity of knowledge. The ideal size of the class depends on the teacher, but I feel that six to eight people is best. Remember that each person will be generating energy, and a comfortable atmosphere needs to be maintained during the class. A first-degree course can be held over one or two days. Traditional Usui Reiki is spread over two days because there are four attunements, with one before lunch and one after lunch each day. Usui Holy Fire Reiki, a refined form of Reiki that is both powerful and gentle, is normally taught in one day, with one attunement and various deep meditations.

Shoden starts the process by enhancing your own personal development. It is designed to remove any emotional or physical blockages that you may have. You will also learn the history of Reiki, the different levels of Reiki, and the way the Reiki attunement works. Reiki is not just a method of healing; it is a way of life, so you will also learn the Reiki principles, which you will find later in this book.

Attunements

Every Reiki teacher has a different way of doing the attunements, but the following should give you a fair idea of what to expect. Normally, students sit in a circle or form an arc with the chairs facing outward. The teacher might give the attunement to the group as a whole, or he might deal with each student in turn. A Reiki Master friend of mine learned Reiki in England and then moved to Japan to study further. He was surprised to find large rooms filled to capacity, in which the Reiki teacher attuned all the students in one go! Mikao Usui himself attuned students by looking at them and sending them the Reiki "intent" in the form of directed energy.

A Reiki teacher will tell the students beforehand what he or she is going to do. Meanwhile, the students sit in a meditation posture called *Gasshô*, which means holding the hands together in a prayer position with the thumbs pointing toward the heart area. Students are asked to close their eyes and to be very quiet and still, as the attunement is carried out in silence.

The Reiki Master connects with the Reiki energy and acts as a channel that links the Reiki energy to the student. The method of visualization, intention, mental and spiritual energy, and the method of connection with the Reiki that each Master uses is a very personal and secret matter. This may vary from one type of Reiki to the next and from one teacher to the next. For instance, some modern teachers like to tap into angelic forces, whereas the more traditional ones link themselves directly to the Japanese Reiki lineage.

Typically, the teacher stands behind each student, then comes to the front of each student and then stands at the back again. He or she may lightly touch the head, shoulders, arms, and hands of each student while focusing on the Reiki energy and bringing it down. Each student is asked to raise his or her hands above the head and hold them there for a few minutes. This ensures the channel stays open in order to link the student to the Reiki energy.

The energy pours into the student through the crown chakra and it flows down from the head to the base of the body. If you aren't familiar with the chakra system, you can find out about it in chapter 8. Other centers that are opened are the spiritual (third) eye, the spiritual heart, and the channel that runs from the heart through the arms to hands. Every time the student gives healing or meditates while linking to Reiki, the energy channels become stronger and allow a greater amount of Reiki to flow through them.

Having said the above, when a friend of mine was attuned for the first time, she found that it was her base chakra that became active first, as she spent days experiencing a weird sensation of heat in her feet and ankles. (The base chakra is often involved in foot and leg matters.) Eventually the Reiki worked its way upward. When she looked into this, she discovered that her experience wasn't unusual. Remember, though, each individual receives and perceives Reiki in his or her own way.

Some students report seeing and feeling colors, lights, or some other strange phenomena, such as feeling heavier than usual. Some will see angels, while others will feel hot, cold, tingly, or even achy. Some will feel very happy and find themselves laughing a little and others will cry a little. Some will get mild cold symptoms for a few days. There are some who won't feel anything at all, but that only means they are on the first steps to spirituality and that it will take a bit of time for their auras to wake up to it all.

The Reiki Master finishes the attunement by sealing the channel of Reiki, and depending upon his or her personal preference, this can be done by using visualization, intention, or Reiki symbols. While waiting for the Reiki Master to deal with other students or while waiting for the session to finish, the students rest their hands on their thighs, palms down, to circulate the Reiki through their bodies.

The Reiki Master may bow to each student or to the group as a whole, perhaps saying *namaste*, which means "I bow to the divine within."

The best approach is to have four attunements over a two-day period, as this allows time for the Reiki to settle in. The attunement has a purifying effect, so any lingering karma or spiritual damage that is within a person will soon go.

A Chanting Method

Another method of attuning students is to chant one of the Reiki *kotodamas* ("power words") during the process, in order to open the student to the quality of the *kotodama* mantra. Yet another is simply to stand among the students and tap into the Mikao Usui lineage and send the students a powerful measure of intention in order to awaken them.

Distant Reiju Empowerment

The word *Reiju* means a blessing or an offering, but in this case, it refers to the passing of the Reiki energy from the teacher to the student.

If it is impossible to get to a session, the attunement can be transmitted to the student in a similar way to that of distant healing. The Master will need to know the specific Reiju empowerments that will open up the energy channels and connect the student to the Reiki, and transmit this over a distance. This isn't ideal, but it is better than nothing. It is also a handy method for students who have received their training but who need to top off their Reiki empowerment from time to time.

Receiving a Distant Reiju Empowerment

To receive the distant Reiju empowerment, you should choose a time when you won't be interrupted. You should sit on a chair or on a big cushion on the ground, as long as this is comfortable for your back.

- Place your hands together in the Gasshô position with the thumbs pointing to the heart.
- Ask for assistance from the Reiki guides.
- Mentally ask to receive the Reiju empowerment. You can even say something like "I am receiving my Reiju empowerment from my Reiki teacher today."
- Relax into the Reiki empowerment and let the feeling flow over your body until you wish to finish, when you need to think "Reiju is ending now" to end the session.
- Place your hands, palms down, on your thighs or against your sides to maintain a connection, and allow the Reiki to flow through your hands and all the channels of your body.
- Stay still and quiet and allow the Reiki to settle in to your system.
- Receive one Reiju empowerment a day for four consecutive days. You may also receive them over two days, one in the morning and one in the evening, and then do the same the next day.

After an Attunement

Once you have received an attunement, you will take part in a group discussion on how you felt about it.

Some students don't get much of a sensation while receiving the attunement, while others do. For instance, it is common to feel tension or dryness in the throat, tingling, or a feeling of serenity. If you seem to be getting a cold, it may well be some of the bad energies in your body being expelled. Don't worry about any of these sensations, but tell yourself that it is normal to react in some way, as it shows the body is responding to the changes the Reiki is bringing about.

If you feel spacey or dizzy after an attunement, focus the mind just below the belly button and place both your palms on your abdomen. Breathe naturally while focusing on this area and feel the abdomen gently moving in and out. If you need more help than this, go outside, take your shoes off, and walk around on grass, allowing the energy to run into the earth beneath your feet until you feel normal again. If you want to take this further you can always try a grounding meditation.

Some Reiki Masters suggest clearing negativity, including bad vibes given out by others, by walking around outside during a new or full moon. My astrologer friends tell me that a new moon is much better, as a full moon can *attract* incoming feelings and emotions from others. Everyone suggests drinking spring water, eating something fresh, such as fruit or salad, going for a walk, and breathing fresh air after an attunement.

❋ ❋ ❋

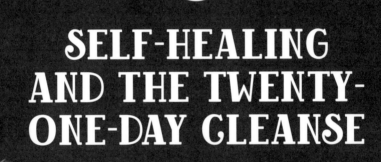

4

SELF-HEALING AND THE TWENTY-ONE-DAY CLEANSE

Before we can heal others, we must heal ourselves, because good fruit does not grow from a sick tree. The first level of Reiki is all about healing ourselves, and the twenty-one-day cleanse after the first Reiki attunement is the start of the process in which we meditate and let go of past wrongs so that we can get to a place where we can heal other people.

Every day, we begin saying the Reiki principles that you will find in chapter 7 so that we change our attitude to life. Finally, we give ourselves Reiki healing, and the more we practice our Reiki healing, the stronger the energy flow will become. The healing energy passes through us, which means that there will be a residual amount of healing energy left in us with every healing we give.

Meditation

Dr. Usui taught a form of meditation called *Gasshô meditation*. The word *Gasshô* means "two hands coming together." This meditation is done by placing your hands together in the familiar prayer position. By bringing the hands together through the palms, we are joining the yin and yang energies, which results in a balanced and calm state of mind.

When we do a Gasshô meditation, the hands are placed in front of the heart chakra while

> ### Tip
>
> By eating and drinking sensibly, we take care of our physical body. By meditating, we help to calm the mind and open ourselves to divine guidance. By giving ourselves Reiki, we guard against illness.

sitting upright in a chair. The important thing is that the spine is kept straight to allow the energy to flow during the meditation. Your head also needs to be kept in an upright position—not too far forward and not too far back. You can place a pillow or cushion at the small of your back to make yourself more comfortable. It is also possible to meditate sitting on the floor, standing with your back supported by a wall, or lying down on a sofa or bed.

- To start, close your eyes with your hands in the Gasshô position and your thumbs touching your heart.
- When you breathe out through your nose, your breath should reach your fingertips.
- Focus your attention on the point where your two middle fingers meet.
- Try to clear your mind. If and when anything comes in, just gently move it out of your mind and return your attention to the point where your two middle fingers meet.
- It may seem that nothing is happening, and that is what meditation is all

about: clearing the conscious mind to allow the subconscious to come forward.

- After fifteen minutes to half an hour, bring your focus back to the room, take a few deep breaths, and open your eyes.

This meditation should be done at the beginning of every Reiki lesson and every morning and evening. It can be done in a group (which increases the energy in the room) or alone. By practicing this meditation every day, you will become more focused and centered in your daily life.

Self-Healing the Mind and Body

To accomplish the self-healing necessary to practice Reiki healing, the mind and body must be healed so that we can change our lifestyle and our reactions to the world. We must come to a place of bodily, mental, and spiritual health. Nearly everyone has moments of sadness or regrets in their past, maybe from childhood when we were most vulnerable and relied on our elders and loved ones to care for us. Pain can even arise from our previous incarnations. These injuries are pushed to the back of our mind or our subconscious. I am not saying it is going to be easy to get past these traumas and forgive those who wronged you, but I am saying it is necessary if you want to live a happy and healthy life. If you think about people who cannot forgive past wrongs, you may also notice that they always seem to be falling ill. Illness feeds on the negative energy of hate and anger; therefore healing starts with self-love and releasing negative feelings from the past.

During the period of self-healing, you can expect periods of illness, including colds, sore throat, or flu-like symptoms. Healing also works on the mind, so your emotions might be all over the place. The mind can only cope with so much emotion, so it will go into overdrive to cope. Don't worry—once you have reprioritized and forgotten what is not needed for your well-being, things will get better. Your relationships with other people may change. When we heal ourselves with Reiki, we bring interpersonal issues to the fore so that they can be healed and forgotten forever. There may be moments of sadness or joy. This is all part of the cleansing process. Of course, not everyone will have problems with the self-healing—some people will not notice any outward change in their lives.

Feeling the Ki

We all have a piece of the divine spark that burns within our hearts, and that flame is the seat of our cosmic consciousness. It is love and compassion in their purest form. When we heal ourselves with Reiki, we feed this fire.

As I have said before, energy is all around us. The *Ki* (energy) that flows in every cell within our body and the Ki that surrounds us in our aura can be charged with the divine, or cosmic, healing energy. Although we cannot see the Ki, we can feel it. The following exercise is used to feel the Ki.

- Sit upright in a chair with your spine straight. Take three deep breaths and relax.
- To sensitize your hands, vigorously rub your palms together (fingers closed) for a few moments. In front of your body, bring both hands close together, leaving a gap of six to eight inches between the palms. After a while, you should feel heat; this is the Ki. If you can't feel the Ki straight away, move your hands closer together and then away again.
- Visualize the Ki between your hands as a ball of light; you can have fun making it bigger or smaller. Then move the ball of energy to the sacral chakra and let it blend with that chakra. (See chapter 8 for more details on chakras.)

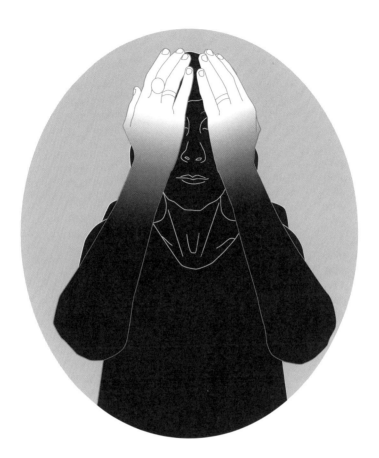

Self-Healing with Reiki

Once you feel the Ki, you are ready to heal yourself (or others when you get to that point). As soon as you put your hands on yourself and think about giving yourself Reiki healing, the thought is the intention. Start with the crown chakra, by putting your hands over your face with the palms on your cheekbones, and work your way down to your feet. This is best done with your eyes closed.

If you're sitting at a table, you can support your arms by resting your elbows on the table. Hold the position for ten to fifteen minutes and then move your hands to the side of your head, just in front of your ears.

Next, you place one hand on your forehead over the brow chakra and one hand on the back of your head.

Then move down to the throat chakra by putting a hand on each side of the throat. I find it easier to cross my arms, but as long as your hands end up in the right position, it does not matter how you got there.

Now move to self-healing the heart chakra, which is one of the most powerful areas for self-healing. Place your hands over your chest, one hand above the other.

From the heart chakra, move down to the solar plexus chakra, just below the sternum (breastbone) and above the belly button. If you are unsure about yourself and your purpose in life, this is where you need to focus self-healing.

The next position for self-healing is the sacral chakra. This area is below the belly button, where we store anger and bitterness. If you have problems with people in authority, this is the area that most needs self-healing.

The final chakra we self-heal is the root, or base, chakra. It is not the easiest place to reach without getting strange looks, so healing is done by placing your hands on your thighs at the top of your legs and visualizing the energy flowing to the base chakra. This chakra provides us with our basic needs; a healthy base chakra allows us to trust that everything will work out. If you are feeling vulnerable or anxious, then you should focus on healing the base chakra.

Other areas that are addressed in self-healing are the knees, ankles, and finally the feet, in order to ground ourselves. To do this, we place our hands on our feet with part of the hands also touching the floor—just like a lightning rod that takes the energy from an electric storm and directs it into the earth.

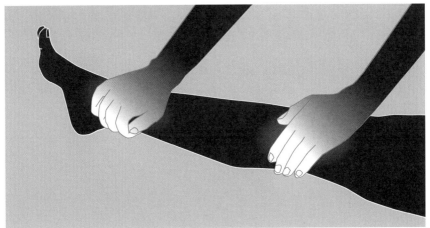

Becoming Overwhelmed

Most Reiki teachers recommend drinking plenty of spring water and avoiding alcohol, coffee, and processed foods at this time. All spiritual work can bring up deep-seated memories and emotions, and you may need to talk these things over with a trusted friend. If you feel overemotional or spacey and light-headed, spend some time out of doors each day walking on grass or on a beach.

✳ ✳ ✳

5

OKUDEN: THE SECOND DEGREE

Once you have completed level one, you can use Reiki on your friends, family, pets, and even your plants, but most people want to widen the scope and move to the next level, Okuden, while some want to set themselves up as Reiki practitioners. There is normally a gap of at least three months between starting level one and going on to level two.

The first couple of hours of a level-two Reiki class serve as a refresher that revisits the things you learned in level one, which is then followed by a guided meditation to connect with Reiki. There is then a talk about the Reiki symbols, after which you will have time to practice drawing them. This is followed by a test on what you have learned so far, including learning how to draw the symbols.

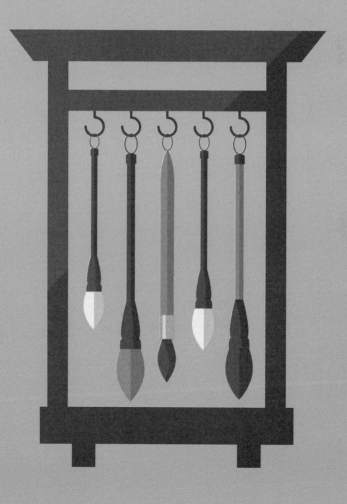

Practicing Reiki

Then students work in pairs to practice healing on each other—still without using the symbols. This is followed by a second attunement and a discussion on how it felt. After a break, students pair up again and give each other Reiki, this time using the symbols. It is common for students to notice that the Reiki energy is much stronger with the symbols than it was without them.

Now the Master explains how distant healing works—and the students practice sending healing to someone who isn't present by using the Reiki symbols.

The Symbols

We are surrounded by symbols that are religious, political, and nationalistic and here are a few that are very familiar:

- The Christian cross is one of the most widely recognized religious symbols, but it was the ichthus (fish) that represented the Christians in the first three centuries CE.

- The wheel of Dharma is one of the most important religious Buddhist symbols; the eight spokes of the wheel symbolize the noble eightfold path set out by Buddha in his teachings.

- The star and crescent is the best-known symbol used to represent Islam. It has been around since ancient times and became associated with Islam during the Ottoman Empire; however, not all Muslims today identify with or use this symbol.

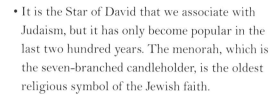

- It is the Star of David that we associate with Judaism, but it has only become popular in the last two hundred years. The menorah, which is the seven-branched candleholder, is the oldest religious symbol of the Jewish faith.

- The most well-known Taoist symbol is the yin-yang symbol, which represents perfect harmonic balance.

With the ubiquitous nature of these symbols, it's no wonder their meaning can sometimes be misunderstood or appropriated for purely fashion-minded reasons, such as the yin-yang symbol that has become a popular design for fashion accessories. Although the Reiki symbols are not as well known as the ones listed above, they are not secret. They are, however, sacred and must be shown respect.

It is believed that the symbols originated in India, and from there they made their way to Tibet, where they were copied by Chinese monks before making their way to Japan. For a long time, these symbols were secrets that were only ever passed on and explained to students by a Reiki teacher. The fact that the symbols are easy to find in books and on the internet doesn't really matter that much, because they have no intrinsic power, as they work only if the healer who is using them has received the Reiki attunement. It is the attunement that empowers the symbols.

Reiki symbols are used to focus the Reiki energy for a specific purpose, for example, healing or protection. The symbols connect directly to our spiritual awareness, so they are our access to higher levels of healing.

Cho-Ku-Rei

Pronounced "cho-koo-ray," this is known as the "power symbol." *Cho-Ku-Rei* means "By divine decree," or "Put the power of the universe here," or "May the Reiki flow here." When you use it, you are invoking a very powerful source of energy and it needs to be given the respect it deserves. This symbol is used before and after each healing session. It is like a key that opens the door for the universal energy to flow. Imagine a voice-activated faucet that instantly allows the healing energy to flow or shut off. The symbol is made over the person being healed at the start of the healing, similar to a priest giving a blessing. It can also be placed in the palm of the healer's hands by tapping the palm three times and saying the name of the symbol, Cho-Ku-Rei, with each tap while visualizing the symbol moving into the hand. In hands-on healing, it is the palm of the hand that the Reiki energy flows from.

Because Cho-Ku-Rei is the most versatile and widely used Reiki symbol, it can be used to cleanse spaces or objects. It is ideal for cleansing food that is served in a restaurant to get rid of any negative energy that may have been

picked up during the preparation of the meal. When you leave your house, you can visualize the symbol sitting next to the door of your home as a form of protection. When your children go to school, the Cho-Ku-Rei can be used to keep them safe from bullying. If you move to a new house, it is a good idea to cleanse each room with this symbol. It is also handy for cleansing objects acquired at a flea market, or what we British call a "car boot sale." It is also a useful symbol to heal negative emotions, thoughts, and attitudes. It is the strongest symbol for personal protection.

The Mantra

If you wish to use this symbol for transcendental meditation, repeat the words "Chu-Ku-Rei" several times.

The Harmony Symbol

This harmony symbol is called *Sei He Ki*, which means "restore balance." It is linked to the heart chakra, which is associated with love, so it brings peace and harmony and it can help the client to calm his emotions and achieve balance.

The Mantra

Repeat the name "Sei He Ki" several times to restore harmony and balance.

Tip

In Reiki we keep our fingers closed while working, whereas with other forms of spiritual healing the fingers are open.

The Distant, or Connecting, Symbol

This symbol, called *Hon-Sha-Ze-Sho-Nen*
which links the healer to whatever God or
powerful deity the healer believes in, such
as Buddha or Christ. It enables the healer to
treat people who are at a distance from him,
but it can also help him to transmit Reiki to a
point in the past or the future.

The Mantra

Repeat the words "Hon-Sha-Ze-Sho-Nen"
as many times as you wish to link you with
those who are far away.

If you are in a public place, you can
visualize yourself drawing the symbols
while silently repeating the names of the
symbols. If working in a space with other
Reiki practitioners, you can put the symbols
around all four walls of the room as well as
the ceiling and floor. However, you shouldn't
display the symbols where they can be seen

Tip

The key to any form of healing is the intent to heal, but when we use the
symbols, our healing abilities are magnified. Each symbol is activated
by drawing the symbol in the air using our dominant hand in front of our
body, saying the name of the symbol three times.

A PERSONAL STORY

I am always amazed by how few people in the medical profession have heard of Reiki. My friend Angie had a red rash and a lump on the midriff area of her body. It was diagnosed as skin cancer and her doctor made an appointment for her to have the lump surgically removed, but she would have to wait six weeks for the operation. It was going to be an outpatient appointment that would take only a couple of hours. On the day the operation was to take place, I drove Angie to the hospital, and after filling out the usual forms, Angie went with the nurse while I settled in the waiting room to listen to some healing music on my iPhone.

After about fifteen minutes, Angie came back. As it happened, when the nurse had started to prepare her for the operation, she noticed the lump had reduced in area and depth since the original consultation six weeks before. The surgeon was called to check the rash and lump and said it would not require surgery as it seemed to be healing on its own. He asked Angie what she'd been doing and she told him she was a Reiki healer, and that every morning at six o'clock she would give herself Reiki healing on the effected area. Neither the surgeon nor any of the nurses had ever heard of Reiki. After a while the rash and the lump completely healed.

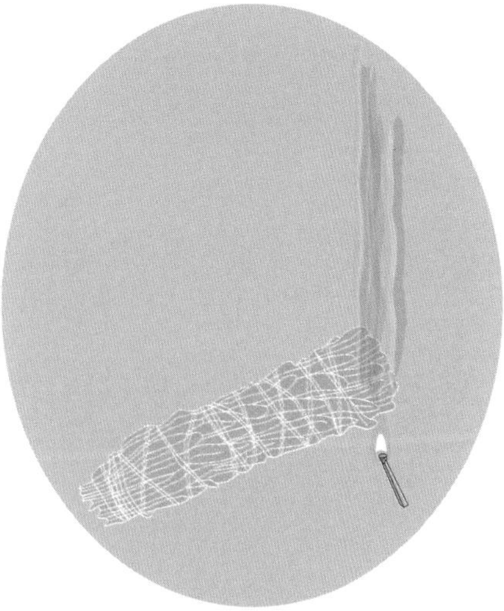

by those who have not been attuned to them.

If you have a Reiki room that is used only for healing, before each healing session you can cleanse the room by burning incense and playing healing music and meditating. Burning white sage is also good for clearing negative energy.

* * *

6

HEALING
OTHERS

Once you have received your second-degree Reiki attunement, you are ready to give healing as a service to your fellow man and animals. In our daily routine, all that is required for the Reiki energy to flow is for us to think about it. The Reiki energy will start to flow as soon as your mind has the intention to heal. Sometimes you may even find that it switches on by itself.

Before we begin to perform Reiki healing on another person, we can check to see if they are in need of any specific healing.

Body Scanning

You can scan for signs of tears in the aura that are symptoms of illness before the illness manifests in the physical body. This is best done while a person is lying on a therapy bed. Place your dominant hand at their crown chakra, then move your nondominant hand slowly down the person's body, with your hand about two or three inches above the body. Feel for any change in the energy field. This may be a change in temperature from one chakra to another, or you may feel the energy spinning more slowly or more rapidly. Like most things, your skills will improve with practice.

Checking for Blockages with a Pendulum

Another way to diagnose problems with the energy flow at the chakras is by using a pendulum, which acts as an extension of your own energy field. Wooden pendulums are best for this type of dowsing. I use a beech wood pendulum that it is pear-shaped and easy to use. The length of the string between the pendulum and your fingers should be six inches, and the pendulum should stay suspended at least two inches from the subject's body. It is important that you clear your mind of all bias as to the state of the chakras.

Tip

There are more Reiki symbols than I have shown in this book, but they are only given to fully trained practitioners.

Tip

Before using the pendulum on another person, it is a good idea to practice with your pendulum through a question-and-answer session so that you can establish how it responds.

With the client lying on his back, start at the base chakra and work your way up the body. An open, healthy chakra will be indicated by the pendulum spinning in a clockwise direction, showing that the chakra is drawing in cosmic energy. Conversely, a counterclockwise movement of the pendulum indicates where blockages are. If you check a blocked chakra again after a Reiki healing session, you should notice a change in the energy flow.

You may also get a left-to-right or forward-and-back movement of the pendulum. Where the chakra is open to receive energy, the pendulum will spin quickly, and with the less open chakras, the pendulum will spin more slowly. Remember that the pendulum is only a tool to help a healer see where there may be problems. (For in-depth knowledge on how to use a pendulum for diagnosing the chakras, I recommend *Hands of Light* by Barbara Ann Brennan.)

HANDS ON OR OFF?

Ask the person you are healing if it is all right to place your hands on his body at certain times. Some practitioners prefer to keep their hands off the body, working only through the aura. Because a healing session typically takes an hour, I find it less tiring to place my hands gently on the body. This also decreases the chance of your hands shaking during healing. It does not matter which method you use, as long as you and the recipient are comfortable during the healing. The important thing is not to try to force the energy from your hands but instead let the client's body draw the healing energy from you.

Beginning a Healing Session

When I begin a healing session, I start with my hands in the Gasshô position and I ask for my guardian angel and my healing guides, the guardian angel and healing guides of the person I am healing, and all past Reiki Masters to assist with the healing.

I draw the power symbol above the person, saying the Cho-Ku-Rei mantra three times. I then repeat the process with the Sei-He-Ki, Hon-Sha-Ze-Sho-Nen, and the Reiki Master symbols. Finally, I tap the symbols into the palm chakras, again saying the mantras three times for each symbol.

This process is called the *Ritual of Intention to Heal*, and it increases the power and flow of the healing energy.

Healing Hand Positions

I start the healing at the crown chakra. Sitting at the head of the bed, I place my hands flat behind the person's ears with my fingers pointing down the sides of the spine. By opening this channel, the energy can travel up and down, to and from the sacral chakra.

This hand position is done by placing the palms on the sides of the head at the temples.

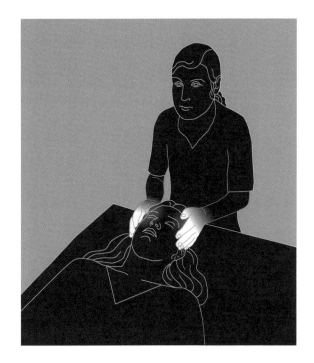

Still around the head, you do the position for healing the third-eye chakra by placing the dominant hand over the forehead; this hand position can be performed while sitting behind or alongside the person.

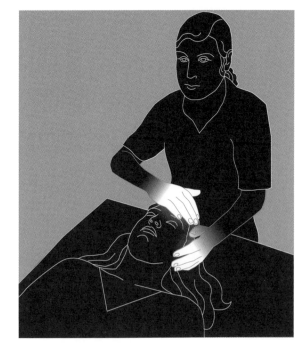

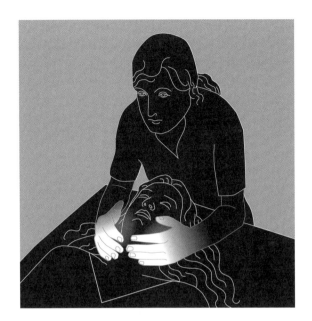

To give Reiki healing to the throat chakra, cup your hands below the chin. You can do this while sitting behind someone and leaning forward or while sitting alongside the person.

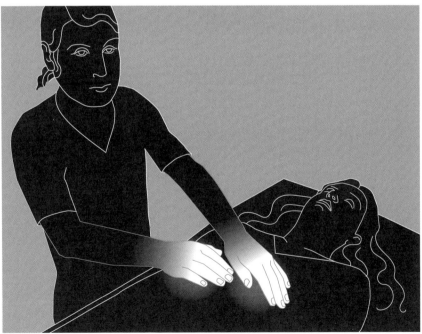

To perform healing on the heart chakra, place your hands over the chest with one hand slightly forward. When healing a woman, place the hands two inches above the chest rather than on the body.

The hand position for healing on the solar plexus chakra is the same as for the heart chakra, with one hand slightly forward, but in the area above the belly button.

To give healing to the sacral chakra, place your hands side by side, just below the belly button.

To give healing to the root (base) chakra, hold your hands about eight inches above the upper thighs and let the Reiki find its own way to where it needs to go.

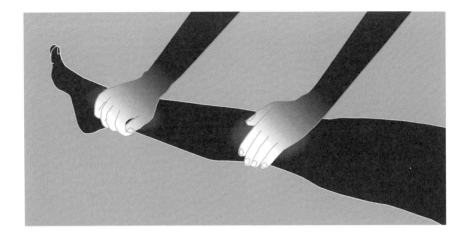

When it comes to the knees and ankles, deal with one leg at a time, as shown in the illustration.

Move to the end of the bed to give some more healing to the feet. I give Reiki to each foot separately by placing my dominant hand on the sole of the foot and my other hand on the arch of the foot.

If there is a difficult area that requires healing, it is ideal to first go over the whole body and then return to give healing to the problem area. Remember that Reiki has a consciousness of its own and goes to where it is needed most.

To end a healing session, you need to ground the person you're giving healing to. To do this, stand at the base of the therapy bed and place your hands on the person's feet. Imagine the negative energy being dragged down the body, from the crown chakra out through the feet, into your hands, up your arms into your heart chakra and down your body, through your legs and feet until it is dispersed into the earth.

When there are two people giving healing, one person is at the shoulders, visualizing pushing the old energy down the body, while the other person is at the feet, directing the negative energy into the ground. Some of my clients have said that they have felt the flow of energy going down their legs.

Ending a Healing Session

Once the healing is complete, move to the center of the therapy bed. Standing over the person, put your hands in the Gasshô position and give thanks to the guardian angels, healing guides, and past Reiki Masters for assisting in the healing. Finally, seal the healing by making a large power symbol over the person, step back, and make a cutting gesture in front of your body with both hands, to detach yourself from the person's aura.

Wash your hands to get rid of any negative energy you may have picked up during the healing. Offer the person a drink of water.

You can talk to the person about how he felt during the healing.

Normally people report having seen colors and felt a sense of peace during the Reiki healing, but sometimes they experience the release of emotions that have been buried for a long time. It is not unusual for people to cry during a Reiki session; it is part of the healing process. That is why I always keep a box of tissues next to the therapy bed.

Explain that the Reiki healing will continue to operate within the body for the next couple of days. Advise them to drink plenty of water to flush away the toxins in the body. Make sure the person is grounded before he leaves and that his chakras are not wide open, especially if he is driving. I once gave a woman a treatment and after the session, we started chatting. She was not fully grounded when she left, and the next time I saw her, she said the healing was amazing, but she had been awake all night!

After the person has gone, it is a good idea to write up some notes, especially if the person is a client. It is always interesting to see how people are progressing.

Healing Children

Where children are concerned, even though Reiki is a gentle, noninvasive form of healing, only those who are properly qualified in Reiki should give it. Never give Reiki or any other form of complementary therapy to children in place of conventional medical attention by a qualified doctor.

A Reiki healer can give Reiki to a child as long as the child understands what's going in and is happy to receive the healing. Having said this, I suggest only giving a short session, or to use distant healing by means of the distant-healing symbol.

All parents know how helpless they feel if their child is sick, so at the very least, this gives a worried parent someone they can turn to who can offer some calm at a bad time.

Healing Animals

Reiki is not a substitute for conventional practice with animals either, so please take your animal to a vet if it is sick, or in the case of large animals, call in a vet if needed. Since Reiki is noninvasive and it can be given in a hands-on manner or by distant healing, it can be given in its own right or in addition to conventional treatment by a vet. Animal Reiki can be administered anywhere, even in a vet's office. It requires no equipment, it doesn't disrupt or upset the animal, and it can't be forced on the animal, as it is up to the animal to decide that it likes the Reiki or to take no notice of it.

If you want to give healing to *someone else's* pet, it is best to go through the training and become qualified before you offer healing. If you want to heal your own

A PERSONAL STORY

◆

Many years ago, I had a Japanese friend who had a long and difficult name, so our family called him Kazoo. One day when Kazoo was staying with us, a blackbird flew into the glass door at the back of the house and landed in a heap on the patio, looking for all the world as if it was dead. Kazoo rushed out and gave the bird Reiki, and to our amazement, it got up on its little feet, shook itself, and flew into the air, doing a circuit of the garden as though thanking Kazoo before flying away.

pet, it's still best to become qualified first, but you can't do much harm, unless you are trying to avoid paying for a visit to a vet.

In the hands of a skilled healer, animals respond well to Reiki, as you will see from the astonishing story above, told to me by my friend Roberta.

A Nice Thought

Because Reiki energy is channeled from a divine source, it flows *through* the healer rather than *from* the healer, so the healer also benefits from the residual energy. The more you practice your Reiki, the stronger it feels.

✻ ✻ ✻

7

THE FIVE REIKI PRINCIPLES AND FURTHER DEGREES

The five Reiki principles were adapted by Dr. Mikao Usui from the principles laid down by Emperor Meiji of Japan (1852–1912) as guidelines for a fulfilled life.

As Reiki practitioners, we follow the center path. This means we live in the real world and accept that we have to deal with everyday problems. We don't hide ourselves in caves on mountains or in tree houses in the middle of the rain forest, or spend our time fasting and meditating all day. That is not to say that fasting and meditating are wrong—both are important in moderation for spiritual development—but they aren't our daily way of life. Nor do we become obsessed with our healing gifts or feed our egos with self-importance, or strive for fame and fortune. Our rewards come irrespective of what we do.

These five principles are normally said first thing in the morning. (I have a laminated copy on my kitchen cupboard.) When I say my Reiki principles, I place my hands in the Gasshô position with both hands together and the fingers touching. When the hands are in this position, the yin and yang energies are balanced. The higher the hands are the more respect is shown. Each principle is repeated three times.

The principles of Reiki are the foundation of who we are as Reiki practitioners. They are a way of life. If and when you fully incorporate them into your day to day, you may wish to go on to more advanced degrees of Reiki—Junshihan and Shihan—which we'll discuss at the end of this chapter.

The First Principle

Just for today, I will let go of anger.

Anger is the most complex inner enemy, and letting go of anger brings peace into the mind. Staying angry at someone for days (or even years) generates a mountain of negative energy that must be climbed daily to keep going. To get past anger, we can make small changes to our thoughts and speech. For instance, I don't use the word *hate*; I prefer to say I "dislike" someone or something.

Note how we say "just for today." We live in the present moment, and tomorrow we can recommit ourselves anew.

There are people who will gladly take advantage of us or act in a way that upsets us, but the anger we feel toward them gives them continuing power over us—sometimes for years. The best way of dealing with angry thoughts is to turn our minds to pleasant ones as soon as the angry ones enter our head. The other person doesn't deserve one iota of our time or consideration, so why give it to him?

As with all "negative" emotions and experiences, there is also a beneficial side, which is that we can learn from them. In this case it means, we will be less inclined to blindly trust in future or to make ourselves believe in someone when we know in our hearts that we are being lied to or used. When anger goes on and on, it becomes corrosive, so we really do need to stop giving brain space to the person who hurt us and move on.

The Second Principle

Just for today, I will let go of worry.

While anger deals with past or present events, worry deals with the future. Some people even worry if everything is going well, because their minds start to invent problems that don't exist. Worry does not change things, and it uses up energy that could otherwise be used to heal.

The positive side of worry is that it shows a sense of responsibility, because only a truly reckless person would go through life without giving consideration to the way things might go in the future. If we have a job that enables us to provide for our family, and we become aware that there are changes afoot in the workplace, of course we will worry. In this case, the worry is the first step to doing something useful, such as starting to look around for another job. Or if you or your partner becomes pregnant when it isn't particularly convenient, well, there is no point in putting your head in the sand about it, because there will soon be a baby to care for. So in this case, too, worry about the future can set us on a course of positive action. However, worrying about things that might *never* happen can be neurotic, and it soon becomes boring and irritating to those who have to live with us. If this kind of worry becomes habitual and a problem, counseling might be in order.

The Third Principle

Today, I will count my many blessings.

No matter how bad things are, there is always something to be grateful for. It may be the people we love or simple things that we take for granted that can make us feel happy. We need shelter, warm clothes, and food, and when you add love to that, life can be perfect.

This is the first *positive* principle, in that it tells us to *do* something rather than to avoid doing something, and in this case, it is a useful concept. Life can be tough at times, and we might get irritated when people tell us there are many others who are in worse positions than we are. We know that. We see them on the news every day, as they struggle with death, starvation, and violence in

> ### Tip
>
> One type of person that it is best to avoid is "the energy vampire." He or she will tell you all their woes and at the end say, "I feel much better now," while you feel drained and worn out. Try to make a person like this turn negative thoughts into positive ones, or you can try to appear to listen without taking anything in.

third-world war zones or gang-ridden countries. However, it is *our* problems that we have to struggle with, and these can come in many forms. But there are always benefits to be found, and sometimes they come from unexpected places.

My friend Frances finds relief from her troubles by spending her spare time puttering around in her tiny garden. She and her family benefit by having lovely flowers to look at and fresh salad and vegetables to eat, and she is always working out what she will grow when the next spring comes around. This proves that there is always something to be grateful for—even if it is only a few compost-filled planters.

The Fourth Principle

Today, I will do my work honestly.

It is a good thing for us to earn a respectable living without harming others or the environment, and we need to support our families. Material possessions are an illusion, though, because we can't take them with us when we pass over to the next life.

This concept means we should do two things: the first is to give a day's work for a day's pay, and the second is to respect the organization that employs us or people who pay us. Firstly, it is important for us to do a good day's work,

because while our efforts might not appear to be noticed, if we start to behave in a slipshod way, that will *definitely* be noticed.

For example, Pete takes a job on a construction site and he turns out to be a capable and competent worker. He keeps at it, taking courses to further qualify him in his trade, and eventually moves up in his line of work. His friend Ethan gets a similar job and he also does well at first, but then he goes out and gets drunk with his friends and he "forgets" to turn up for work for the next couple of days. The first time he does this, he gets away with it, but the second time it happens, the supervisor fires him.

The Fifth Principle

Today, I will be kind to every living creature.

We are all connected through the universal life force energies, to everything that is on this planet and everything within the cosmos. Some people decide to be vegetarian, but if you don't want to give up meat, then before you eat, at least give thanks to the animal that has given its life for your benefit.

Being kind to every living creature is almost impossible for anyone other than a saint. I find it heartbreaking when I hear of cruelty and neglect to children, the elderly, and animals, because vulnerable people and animals depend upon us. However, what about spiders? Well, some of us do catch

them and toss them outside. Great! But do we do the same with mice, cockroaches, flies, mosquitoes, and columns of ants that march into our kitchens? Of course not. I guess there has to be a happy medium here, because the health and safety of our loved ones comes first—and so does common sense.

However, where other humans are concerned, a little kindness can go a long way. Lending a helping hand to an elderly neighbor can make her day a little better. If we want to give back to the community, perhaps we can find a local charity, and offer hands-on help as well as a little of our money. That might be even turn out to be good fun.

This might be enough Reiki training for now, but if you later decide to take things further, you can go on to degrees three and four.

SERVING OTHERS

Healing is a service to our fellow beings. To serve others we have to be prepared to metaphorically "walk without shoes," which means that we have to be humble, while ignoring those who criticize our way of life.

We all have egos, and some people have feelings of self-importance that get in the way when it comes to healing. The best way to heal others is to first heal ourselves, and some of this can be achieved by letting go of ego. It is better to let others sing our praises than to sing them ourselves. So go about your healing with a kind and loving heart, earning a reasonable fee for sure, but without seeking fame or fortune.

KI MEDITATION

The *Ki* (energy) flows in every cell within our body, and the Ki that is in our auras can be charged with divine, or cosmic, healing by energy using this meditation. As your Reiki practice deepens and you incorporate the five Reiki principles into your everyday life, it's a good idea to recharge your Ki every so often. If you're ever feeling drained or just want to give yourself a boost before or after a healing session, you can use this energizing meditation:

- Sit upright in a chair with your spine straight. Have a footstool positioned in front of you.

- Take three deep breaths and relax.

- Vigorously rub your palms together with the fingers closed for a few moments, keeping your hands front of your body. Bring both hands close together, leaving a gap of six to eight inches between the palms.

- After a while, you should feel warmth. This is the Ki. If you can't feel the Ki right away, move your hands closer together and then away again, and you will start to feel a resistance, almost as though there is a balloon between your hands.

- Visualize the Ki between your hands as a ball of light; you can have fun making it bigger or smaller.

- Now move the ball of energy to the sacral chakra and let it blend with that chakra.

- Place your feet on the footstool.

- Hold one hand about two or three inches over your feet and start to move it around.

- You will soon feel the aura that comes off your feet while your feet will tingle a little as your hands pass over them.

- When you have had enough fun with this, hold the Ki energy in your hand and bring it up to the solar plexus chakra. Allow the energy to be absorbed into your aura, body, and chakra.

- Gently come back to the world, relax your hands, and open your eyes.

MY EXPERIENCE

There are many different forms of Reiki, and I started by learning traditional Usui Tibetan Reiki up to the level of Master/Teacher, which is still the most practiced form of Reiki in the West. Then I studied Karuna Reiki, which has an emphasis on love and compassion. Karuna Reiki uses more Reiki symbols than Tibetan Reiki, and it focuses on meditations that help the student connect with spiritual guides and archangels.

It was from here that I was spiritually directed to become a Usui Holy Fire Reiki Master/Teacher. Along with six other Reiki Masters, I received my Usui Holy Fire Reiki Master/Teacher attunement during a weekend retreat at Chalice Well, which is situated at the foot of Glastonbury Tor in Somerset, England.

Prior to the start of the course we were advised to fast for a week and break the fast the day before the course with a light meal. There would be no connection with the outside world during the retreat, and cell phones were not allowed. The night after the first day, when we received a Holy Fire initiation, I had the strangest dream. I saw a cup that was flowing over and the contents were pouring into a bigger cup, but that cup could not hold the contents so it also flowed over. It was as if we were receiving an abundance of love and compassion to drink from.

When I returned to my healing practice and started using Holy Fire Reiki, my clients noticed the difference between the healing energies that I had used before and the new one that had come in. That is not to say one form of energy is better than another, because all healing comes from the same source.

This might be enough Reiki training for now, but if you later decide to take things further, you can go on to degrees three and four.

Third Degree: Junshihan

This is the advanced training for a potential Reiki Master/Practitioner. It is normally a one-day training course during which you will receive the Usui Master symbol and the Usui Master attunement. This will increase the strength of your Reiki energy, and you will also be able to use the Master symbol in healing.

You will also learn how to charge crystals with Reiki, make a Reiki grid using crystals, and perform psychic surgery and aura clearing. Aura clearing will allow you to remove negative psychic energy from your clients and send it to the light.

This third level—also known as Advanced Reiki Training (ART) or Master Practitioner—is usually combined with the fourth level, a Reiki Master/teacher class, but it can be done on its own if the student does not wish to become a Master or teacher.

Holy Fire

If you are taking a Holy Fire course, you will also learn the Holy Fire symbol and receive the Holy Fire ignitions and Holy Fire meditations.

Fourth Degree: Shihan

This is the three-day Master/Teacher course, which includes advanced Reiki training. It is an intensive course in which you review all you have learned in your previous Reiki training and also receive the Usui Master symbol and the Usui Master attunement. A large part of the time will be spent practicing ways of giving Reiki attunements for all levels of Reiki.

❋ ❋ ❋

8

CHAKRAS
AND
CHANNELS

The word *chakra* means "wheel" in the ancient language Sanskrit, the primary liturgical language of Hinduism. There are seven main chakras and twenty-one minor chakras in the body. Two of the minor chakras are in the palm of the hands, but they are important for hands-on healing. It is also through the hands that we get an impression of someone when we shake their hand for the first time.

Chakras are spinning energy transformers that are capable of shifting energy to higher and lower vibrations. The flow of energy around the body is in harmony when our chakras are balanced and spinning correctly. If we have a blockage in one of our chakras, the flow of energy is disrupted and illness develops, be it physical or emotional. In Reiki, we work with chakras to clear blockages and get healthy energy to flow.

The vibration of energy changes as we move up the chakras, with the base chakra being the densest and the crown chakra being the lightest.

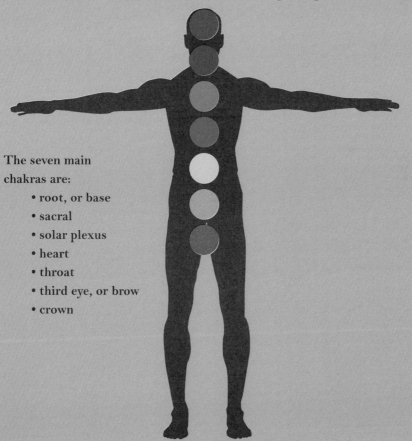

The seven main chakras are:

- **root, or base**
- **sacral**
- **solar plexus**
- **heart**
- **throat**
- **third eye, or brow**
- **crown**

The seven chakras were not taught by Dr. Usui, but were adapted into the modern system of Reiki in the 1980s with the advent of the New Age movements. The original Japanese Reiki focused on the three diamonds of Earth Ki, Heaven Ki, and Heart Ki.

The Earth Ki, also known as the *hara*, is three inches below the belly button and contains the energy we are born with. It connects us to the Earth and is important for grounding. The Heaven Ki is located at the forehead and is used for visualization and spiritual connection. The Heart Ki, as the name suggests, is at the heart, and it is used to balance the Earth Ki and the Heaven Ki. These three energy points are commonly used in meditation and martial arts.

Adding Indian chakras to the Reiki system has allowed for direct healing to specific locations. Each chakra is connected not only to the physical body but also to the emotional and spiritual body. As a Reiki healer, it is important to know where each chakra is and which organs and emotions they are associated with.

FEELING THE CHAKRAS

To practice feeling the chakras, have a friend or family member sit upright on a stool. Sensitize your hands by rubbing them together. To feel the heart chakra, use the dominant hand—the one you write with—and place it with the palm facing the heart, about two inches away from the body. Place your other hand at the back of the person, aligned with their heart, again with your palm facing the body, and about two inches away from it. If you have trouble feeling the chakra, move your hands around so that they move away from the body and back toward it. Think of your hands like two funnels joined together with their spouts at the center of the chakra. Once you are happy with your ability to feel the heart chakra, you can practice feeling for the other chakras using this same method.

The Root (Base) Chakra
Hindu Name: *Muladhara*
Ruling Element: Earth
Color: Red

The root chakra is situated at the perineum between the genitals and the anus. It points down, and, as its name suggests, it is what connects us to the Earth. Just as a tree has roots connecting it to the earth and supporting it, the root chakra is the support that we require to help us grow and develop.

When we are born our chakras are closed, and they open in seven-year cycles starting with the root chakra. The root chakra is associated with the material things that we need for survival, such as food, drink, and shelter. Up to the age of seven, we rely on our parents or guardians to provide these basic needs, and it is from them that we get our security and physical well-being that will shape us as we grow into adulthood. If we come from a stable and secure background that is filled with love and approval, we feel secure, which makes us outgoing, confident, and reliable. If, on the other hand, we have to fight to survive and are made to feel that we are a burden to our parents or guardians, this can lead to disruptive behavior that may manifest in violence, being judgmental or fearful, or needing to accumulate unnecessary material possessions. These negative issues can be healed, but they need to be addressed and shown the light of day before they can be mended.

The Sacral Chakra
Hindu Name: *Svadhishthana* ("our abode," "dwelling place")
Ruling Element: Water
Color: Orange

The sacral chakra is situated about a hand's width below the belly button, and it is known as the creativity and sexual chakra. It starts to open between the ages of seven and fourteen, and includes the age of puberty, when we begin to explore the world around us and learn our place in it both emotionally and physically.

HAVING IT ALL

◆ ◆ ◆

I knew a man who looked as if he had everything. He got a new, trendy car each year, because he thought that this would attract pretty women. As soon as the latest phone or new gadget appeared on the market, he had to have it. He was a totally materialist person and eventually married a woman who was just like him. She had a high-paying job and a teenage son from a previous marriage. The man did not want children of his own and had never had to share anything with another person. Their relationship became a competition to see who could spend the most money. Her job meant that she had to travel a lot, and she soon found someone else and left him. He could not understand why she had wanted a divorce and wondered if things might have been different if they had had a child together.

As it turned out, the man was just like his father, who also placed too much value on material things. When the man found another woman to love, this new relationship did not last long either, because he thought of the woman as just another possession—he was not capable of real love. He was very concerned about what others might think of him and he judged others by his own standards. He believed that living in a big house and having plenty of money would make him happy, but despite having these things, he was a very unhappy man. He could not find love because he was looking in the wrong place and was unwilling to share.

This is when we are encouraged to develop our own personality and form relationships. We learn to share and are happy in the company of others. When there is imbalance in the sacral chakra, we can feel jealousy, a fear of sexuality or an uninhibited desire, and a lack of creative energy. We can help to balance this chakra in others by giving them confidence in themselves, by encouraging self-belief and self-worth, and by showing them they are worthwhile members of society. When children worry about something that might seem trivial to us, we should realize that it is a major problem for them and treat it accordingly. We should also highlight the things that they are good at and stop them from focusing on their weaknesses. This will help them see the glass as half full rather than half empty.

The Solar Plexus Chakra

Hindu Name: *Manipura* ("the place of jewels")
Ruling Element: Fire
Color: Yellow

The element of fire rules the solar plexus chakra, and in alchemy, fire is the element into which base metals are placed to transform them into gold. This chakra is located above the belly button and starts to open at fourteen years of age and becomes fully open at about twenty-one. This is our power center and the seat of our emotions; it is also the home of the ego. It is in the solar plexus chakra that we develop into a unique individual who stands apart from others. As it opens, we at last become ready to leave the safety of the nest and make our way in the world. The ego is an important part of our ability to function in the wider world. We can use our ego to connect with others in a loving and caring way, or we can use our ego to control and dominate others. When we hurt others, or when we are hurt by someone we care about, we get that sick feeling in our stomach, which is an emotional response that manifests in the solar plexus chakra.

When this chakra is balanced, we have an air of authority, we are good at organizing things, and we have natural leadership qualities. If the solar plexus chakra is out of balance, we can become rebellious and stubborn.

Lower and Upper Chakras

The root, sacral, and solar plexus chakras are lower, or earthbound, chakras, but as we move to the upper chakras, which are the heart, throat, third-eye, and crown chakras, we move into the realms of spirituality, divine development, and our spiritual journey. People often focus on the upper chakras because they want to connect to their real or spiritual self, but it is just as important to look after the lower chakras, because if we don't pay attention to them, we can lose touch with our roots—just as a tree or flower needs good soil for it to bloom and flourish.

The Heart Chakra

Hindu Name: *Anahata* ("unhurt")
Ruling Element: Air
Color: Green

The heart chakra is the healing center of our being, and it is where the energy of the lower and higher chakras meets. The soul resides in our heart rather than in our head. When we connect with the divine energy, it comes in through our crown chakra, then down through the third-eye and throat chakras before resting in the heart chakra. In hands-on healing it is from the heart chakra that the healing energy flows across our chest, down our arms, and into the recipient via the palms of our hands. (We can also use our eyes to beam healing energy—or our mind to send distant or remote healing.)

The heart chakra is where we connect with our fellow beings through love and compassion. It is where we bond with others and form deep friendships and intimate relationships. When we lose someone we love, it feels like a void in the heart, and this feeling of loss takes time to heal. An open heart allows our true nature to emerge and reveal itself. Some people wear their hearts on their sleeves. Others keep their heart protected and show the world only what they want other people to see. The breakup of a relationship and loss of love can cause us to retreat into ourselves and put up a barrier that stops us from loving again. Sometimes the fear of revisiting that level of pain is stronger than the joy that love can bring into our lives, but once we have experienced love with an open heart, we always want to feel it again. Reiki can heal that fear and open the heart to that love when it returns.

To love others with an open heart starts with loving yourself, but there is a difference between self-love and vanity. I remember when I was working as a bartender in a pub, there was a young man who used to come in regularly and sit on a stool facing the mirror behind the bar. Whenever he thought no one was looking, he would turn his head to admire his reflection. That is vanity. Self-love is more about self-worth, because if you don't love yourself for who you are, how can you expect anyone else to love you? And if you suffer from low self-esteem, you need to remind yourself how good and kind you are.

The Throat Chakra

Hindu Name: Vishuddha ("very pure," "purification")
Ruling Element: Ether
Color: Light Blue

The throat chakra is situated at the base of the neck and is associated with the thyroid gland. The second layer of the aura (see chapter 9 for more on the layers of the aura) is called the "etheric auric body" and is associated with the throat chakra. The etheric value is that of vibration, and sound is a form of vibration that can be used for communication. We use the throat chakra to express ourselves, as a means of telling others what we feel and think. We don't only use the throat chakra to express ourselves; we also receive vibrations through this chakra. For example, if we see or hear something that stirs our emotions, we get a lump in our throat.

This chakra is between the mind, which sees things in a practical way, and the heart, which relies on emotions, so sometimes there is a conflict in this area. People with balanced throat chakras are confident and articulate, whereas those who have a blockage in the throat chakra have problems expressing themselves. They may tend to swallow and stammer, they are easily influenced and misled by others, and their creativity can is often dampened.

The Third-Eye, or Brow, Chakra

Hindu Name: *Ajna* ("perceive")
No Ruling Element
Color: Dark Blue

The third-eye chakra is situated between the eyebrows and linked to the pineal gland, which is sometimes called the seat of the soul. This gland produces hormones that modulate sleep patterns. The third-eye plays a role in our spiritual development and our communication with spiritual beings.

The third eye is where we receive our intuition, which may come in the form of dreams, visions, clairvoyance, or telepathy. Spiritual awareness and visions are sometimes preceded by bright lights. When the third-eye chakra is open, we get insight into who we really are on a spiritual level and we are open to gaining access to occult knowledge. If there is a blockage or imbalance in the third-eye chakra, then we refuse to learn life's lessons and display pessimism or confusion. It is through the third eye that energy ascends and descends to and from the crown chakra.

The Crown Chakra
Hindu Name: *Sahasrara*
No Ruling Element
Color: Violet or Gold

The crown chakra is located at the top of the head where the skull bones meet. This chakra points up and is the gateway to our spiritual enlightenment, or cosmic consciousness. It has sometimes been referred to as the "God source."

Just as the base chakra connects us firmly to the Earth like a plant, the crown chakra is the flower that reaches for the sky. In Hindu and Buddhist traditions, the crown chakra is seen as a thousand-petal lotus. The lotus flower has its roots in muddy water but the flower blooms in the light.

When the crown chakra is closed or is out of balance, we are stuck in the material world, unable to connect to our higher, spiritual self. We become attached to possessions and unable to let go of material things. We become dissatisfied with what we have and complain about the world around us, becoming set in our ways and believing that we are right and disregarding other people's opinions.

When we connect with the higher self and divine spirit, there is a sense of peace and calm. We feel whole and loved. To open the crown chakra, we only need to relax, let go of all earthly thoughts, and accept the love that is our birthright from our creator.

Energy Channels

Within the physical body there are three main energy channels: the *sushumna*, *ida*, and *pingala*. The *sushumna* channel runs vertically up the spine from the base chakra to the crown chakra. At each end of these chakras we are connected to the earth (base chakra) and spirit (crown chakra). There are two holes on either side of the spine, which are like conduit pipes that nerves pass through. These are the *ida* and *pingala*, the left and right channels. They represent the masculine and feminine energy, or yin and yang. As the energy from the *ida* and *pingala* spirals up the body they cross over at each of the major chakras until they reach the third-eye chakra, where they merge with the energy from the *sushumna* channel. In the *sushumna* we become aware of an inner balance where no matter what is going on around us we don't let it disturb us, so this brings inner peace.

The Nadis

Linked to the chakras are the *nadis*, of which there are 72,000. These channels are also known as meridians, and they carry energy to all parts of the body, providing energy to the major organs and living tissues. The energy is negative and positive, or yin and yang. It is along these channels that acupuncture is carried out and reflexologists direct their healing energies.

9

THE AURA

The human aura is a colorful, multilayered electromagnetic field of energy that emanates from and surrounds the body like a halo. It is connected to and gets its various colors from the chakras. The different layers also have various energy densities and connect us to our surroundings. Think of the aura like an antenna that you can use to transmit your own feelings as well as receive other people's. When we meet someone, we connect with their aura for a while. This is why we sense that some people seem to have a healthy radiance about them while others seem sick and lethargic. Our innate sense of the auras of other people helps us navigate everyday life.

The aura is an indication of a person's physical, mental, and spiritual energies, so the bigger and stronger the aura, the healthier the person. Everything has an aura, including rocks, plants, and animals, but while animals are sensitive to auras, normally only people who are psychic can see auras. With practice, however, you will at least be able to sense them as a haze around a person's body. Sometimes there may be a tear in the aura that allows energy to escape—Reiki can heal these lacerations.

Halos

········◆◆◆◆◆◆◆········

Ancient pictures show holy men and women with halos around their heads. This is a representation of the aura.

Aura Colors

········◆◆◆◆◆◆◆········

Red = anger
Green = love and healing
Violet or gold = spirituality

There is a method of photographing auras called *aura imaging*. This is done by placing your left hand on a special biosensor that has various contact points linked to a camera and computer software. The biosensor detects your temperature and electrodermal activity, or electrical impulses. The computer then takes that data and works with the camera to capture a photographic representation of your aura. These aura photographs can be used to help you see issues in your chakras.

High-tech methods aside, the best way to see an aura is to ask a friend to stand against a plain background—a painted wall is ideal. Then, from about five or six feet away, stare at your friend and allow your eyes to slip out of focus. Let the shape of your friend's head, shoulders, and upper body imprint onto your retina. Close your eyes. You will see your friend's outline clearly, and you may see colors swirling around the outline. With practice, you should be able to pick up the aura.

The Physical Auric Body

The first layer of the aura, which is the one that is closest to the physical body, is the physical auric body. This is linked to the base chakra and is associated with physical sensations and comfort. It extends from about a quarter inch to two inches beyond the physical body. Because this layer of the aura is close to the physical body, Reiki healers can tap into it to determine the vitality of the flow of energy around a person.

Psychics can see this as a red color, but it doesn't actually mean that the person is feeling angry or upset, just that it is associated with the base or root chakra.

The Etheric Auric Body

The second aura layer is the etheric auric body, which is less dense than the first layer. It is linked to the sacral chakra and to feelings such as love, excitement, joy, or anger. It is orange in color and extends between one inch and three inches from the body. This energy field is affected when we are depressed or in conflict with others.

The Emotional Body

The third auric layer is the emotional body, and it is finer still in density. It connects to the solar plexus chakra and is where the rational mind can be observed. Emotions such as anger, fear, or regrets from the past are held in this energy field. This auric layer should have a golden yellow color, but if we get irritated or angry, it can become red for a while. The first three layers of the aura are called the *physical plane*.

The Astral Level

The fourth auric layer is the astral level, which is where we interact with other people. It is connected to the heart chakra because it is on this level that we communicate our feelings to those we are attracted to. This is where the energy fields of two people who are compatible talk to each other. Our energies of spiritual growth and love originate here. This layer extends from six inches to one foot from the body. The normal color for this layer is green, but it can change according to a person's mood or state of health.

The Etheric Template

The fifth layer of the aura is the etheric template, which is linked to the throat chakra and extends up to one and a half feet from the physical body. This blue layer is where our uniqueness and identity are felt. It is also how we connect to the divine aspects of our being as it guides us to speak and follow the truth.

The Third-Eye Aura

The sixth layer of the aura is associated with the third-eye chakra. It is from here that we can connect to God or the divine, through which unconditional love is felt. It is indigo in color and extends from two to two-and-a-half feet from the body. It also has a group consciousness whereby we can share the divine love.

The Ketheric Template

The seventh layer, the ketheric template, links with the crown chakra. This extends from two-and-a-half to three feet from the physical body. It should glow with a purple hue, but like all parts of the aura, the color can change according to the person's mental, emotional and physical condition. This is where we connect to our real self and the way that we fit in with the greater scheme of things and because this layer is also a connection to spiritual, if we are too open, we may lose connection with the Earth.

AURIC EXTENSION

Although the aura normally radiates out about three feet from the physical body, it can extend much farther depending on the energy and the spiritual condition of the person. Before you enter a room, your aura may already have connected with those on the other side of the door, leading you to places to which you feel intuitively drawn.

❈ ❈ ❈

10

ANGELS
AND GUIDES

Angels and angel-like figures appear in nearly all major religions, where they play the important role of God's messengers. Angels can disguise themselves as humans when they wish, but angels are not, and have never been, human. They are ageless and sexless, and they can make themselves visible or invisible. It is a common belief that when we are born, we are assigned a guardian angel who helps us and protects us throughout our life, and who is there to help us cross over to the other side of the veil when we die.

Above the legions of angels are the archangels. During the second century BCE, Enoch described his visit to heaven, and this is the first time we hear the names of the seven archangels: Michael, Gabriel, Raphael, Uriel, Raguel, Saraqael, and Remiel. Archangel Michael is the best known of the archangels, but it is Raphael who is important to Reiki, as he is the angel of healers. The name *Raphael* means "shining one who heals."

Angels

••••••••◆◆◆◆◆••••••••

You may notice that the name of each archangel ends with *el*, and many Reiki teachers think this suffix means "shining being" but it does not. El is a very ancient Aramaic word that stands in place of the name of God. Many ancient Hebrew blessings call on *elohenu*, meaning "our lord" or "our God," and it even turns up in the word *Israel*.

Angels and Guides in Reiki

Although not part of the practice taught by Dr. Usui, spirit guides and angels are now firmly part of Reiki healing, and there is even a form of angelic Reiki. The angelic Reiki attunement is not done by the Reiki Master, and the energy does not come through the teacher. The attunement is done by the angelic kingdom of light, and it is given to the student as a gift by his or her own healing angel. This kind of attunement, also known as "ignition," comes as a result of meditating on the third heaven, and because of this direct link to the third heaven, and the beings of pure light, it is a stronger form of energy. This is not specific to angelic Reiki, however, as it is also common in Karuna Reiki, where by one connects with the angelic realms and, in particular, the archangels.

In Holy Fire Reiki you are taken on a guided meditation to the "ocean of holy love," which is an ocean of liquid light that contains many colors and frequencies that provide healing for a wide range of conditions and issues. There is also a "heavenly banquet hall experience."

There is a powerful meditation Reiki healers can do that activates and connects us to the gifts, qualities, and essence of the archangels of the Tree of Life. A link is also created to the healing qualities of the crystals of the mythical city of Atlantis so that the gifts may be used. You will find information about crystal healing in chapter 12. In angelic Reiki at the Master level, the recipients are first attuned to the gifts of twelve symbols. The symbols are activated to the Master's angelic level. In a second attunement, the symbols are activated to the galactic level by Lord Melchizedek. As part of the archangelic initiation, the symbols are activated to their subatomic, molecular, genetic, mathematical, musical, physical, and super-luminary aspects. As in Usui Reiki, all angelic Reiki attunements are preceded by a cleansing period.

Tip

Because angels come from the third heaven, they do not have egos. Spirit and healing guides, on the other hand, do have egos.

Meeting Your Guide—A Meditation

During my Reiki training I was led on a visualized meditation by my Reiki master/teacher to a temple where I might meet my guide. This is how such a meditation works:

- You are walking down a country lane, feeling the earth beneath your feet.

- You come to a field with a gate.

- Go through the gate to a path that leads through a field.

- In the distance there is a plateau with a building on it.

- In the far distance there are snow-covered mountains.

- As you cross the field, you can feel the earth beneath your feet and you become aware of the scent of the flowers and any wildlife you meet.

- At the bottom of the plateau there are steps. You climb up these steps, noting the material they are made from.

- At the top of the plateau there is a temple. Notice what it is constructed from.

A PERSONAL STORY

Recently I received spiritual healing from Brian, a six-foot-tall, ex-army physical training instructor who also gives body massages in addition to healing. I felt a powerful energy emanating from his hands when he reached my knees. I soon felt his hands on my feet grounding me, but I could still feel both his hands on my knees at the same time. Both sets of hands felt different, one being male and the other female. I thought someone else had joined us and was helping with the healing, so I opened my eyes to find it was only Brian giving healing. It isn't uncommon for people to feel more than one set of healing hands during a Reiki healing session.

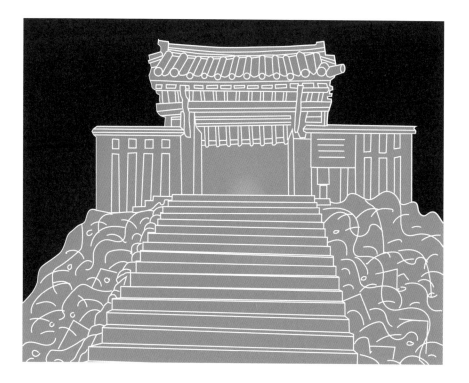

- There is a door that is slightly open, so you enter.

- Is it dark or is it light inside the temple?

- Is there an altar in the room?

- Is there a gift for you on the altar?

- Is there anyone else present, and if so do they introduce themselves to you?

- When you have finished exploring the room and meeting anyone there, give thanks for your gift and bid farewell to your guide.

- Go back through the door and make your way down the steps, across the field, through the gate, and into the lane to make your return journey.

Some Reiki healers are also shamanic or spiritual healers who can connect with their guides with ease. Personally, I did not meet my guide in the temple, which for me is always a cave with a rough stone altar, but while I was there, I did feel the presence of someone standing behind me. I continue to sense a guiding presence in my life, and I know when there is an angel around me, because I feel their wings around me like a heavy coat that is being placed around my shoulders to keep me warm.

Healers don't always see their guides, but when I give healing to someone who is psychic, *they* see someone in the room during the healing, and I have been told it is a tall Chinese man standing next to me. Once, when receiving healing from a person who is very aware, she told me there was a tall South American who appeared to be an Aztec warrior standing by my side, and she asked him if he was one of my guides. He replied that he was one of my protectors.

Grounding

I mentioned in a previous chapter, meditation can make you feel a little dizzy or slightly disoriented, and the same goes for working with such powerful energy forms as Reiki. Spiritual energy tends to link us to the heavens and the universe, so when working in this way, we need to balance this with some earth energy. A good way of obtaining earthy energy is by carrying out a grounding meditation, such as the one below. It has the secondary benefit of clearing your mind and heart of anxiety and restlessness.

Grounding Meditation

Sit down on a comfortable chair in a quiet place where nobody will interrupt you. There is no need to hold your hands upward or in any special position, just make sure you are comfortable.

- Close your eyes and relax.

- Focus on breathing in a regular way. Keep on concentrating on your breathing while you relax.

Helpful Hints

Another way to ground yourself walk around in the fresh air, especially in an area where there are plants, trees, and greenery around. Another great place to walk is by a lake or on the seashore. If possible, go barefoot for a while, but take care not to hurt your feet or let them get cold or wet. If you can't walk around outdoors, take a few leaves from a tree and hold them in your hand, as this will also ground you a little, but don't forget to thank the tree for letting you help yourself to its leaves.

• Once you feel relaxed, become conscious of your feet on the ground and imagine your feet have roots. Now imagine the roots going deep into the ground.

• Let the roots grow deeper into the ground, until they link with the center of the earth.

• Imagine the base of your spine lengthening and growing downward, until it also reaches deeply into the earth.

• Let all your worries and fears flow away down these roots, taking your troubles away into the cleansing earth.

• Allow feelings of love and positivity flow upward from the earth through the roots, into your heart and soul.

• Gradually come back to the world and open your eyes.

Have a drink of water, and then dawdle for a bit without immediately rushing around and doing chores. Give yourself time to unwind.

❋ ❋ ❋

11
HEALING ACROSS SPACE AND TIME

In the universal field of energy, we are all connected and separation is an illusion. Although we appear to be individual, we are part of the larger divine being—God, Supreme Being, it does not matter which name you choose. It is our ego that makes us think we are separate.

Many people believe that when a certain number of beings achieve awareness of something, this new awareness may be communicated from mind to mind through the universal energy field. There is a story, commonly known as the "hundredth monkey effect," about a scientific study of macaque monkeys on the Japanese island of Koshima in 1952. The researchers observed that some of the younger monkeys would wash their sweet potatoes before eating them. This new behavior spread through the younger generation of monkeys, and when it reached the hundredth monkey, some say that the same behavior spread to the nearby islands, although no physical contact took place with the other groups.

Could this type of communication explain how ancient civilizations in Egypt and South America built similar-shaped pyramids on the opposite sides of the planet long before worldwide travel?

Distance Healing

When Jesus said "Love your neighbor as yourself" and "Do unto others as you would have them do unto you," maybe it was his way of telling us we are all one. It is through the interconnectedness of the universal energy field that Reiki healing over great distances is possible. The ability to send Reiki healing instantly to someone or some situation anywhere in the world is becoming more important than ever. Nearly every week, I am asked to send healing to someone. As part of a spiritual group, we often arrange to send healing at the same time on a particular night, because twenty people sending healing to the same person at the same time amplifies the healing energy.

There are thoughts that have a lasting effect on others and on us—the thoughts that can change our futures. They are like seeds that find fertile soil in our minds and the minds of others. These are the thoughts that take spiritual shape within our soul and body. Once the thought is given life, it cannot die, and we who give these thoughts life are responsible for their outcome. Each of these thoughts has the potential for good or evil. Evil or negative thought is like a virus, which when it finds a host, is given manifestation and substance in order to transfer the thought into action. We should try to avoid negative thoughts, and it is better to say we dislike something than to say we hate it. Fortunately, good, positive thoughts allow us to send healing energy into the universe, regardless of distance.

One of the most well-known cases of distant healing is in the Bible, when Jesus heals the nobleman's son and the centurion's servant. The centurion had

faith in Jesus, and he knew that it was not necessary for Jesus to come to his home to visit the sick servant; His word was sufficient to heal, whether near or far.

In England, one of the best-known healers was Harry Edwards (1893–1976). He was also a hands-on spiritual healer who once gave a public healing demonstration in the Royal Albert Hall in London, in front of six thousand people. At his healing sanctuary, he would receive between nine thousand and eleven thousand letters a week requesting distant healing.

Tip

Some people believe that the power of love, which has energy of its own, vibrates and affects every cell in the body. The wave frequency of love can be felt and has been shown to immediately increase hormones like oxytocin, endorphins, and antioxidants that assist cellular repair.

The ideal way to send distant healing is to arrange for the healing to take place at a certain time. I like to do mine at nine o'clock at night, because most of the daily chores are complete and people are usually relaxed, making them open to receiving healing. If possible, the conditions should be mirrored by both recipient and healer as much as possible. I usually light a candle and dim the lights, and play some healing music, and I recommend that my client do the same. It is not unusual for the person receiving the healing to fall asleep during the healing, and this is no problem, as the person will still receive the healing. As with hands-on healing, it is the *intention* to heal that is important.

It helps if you have a photograph of the person to be healed and a description of the illness, but the least that is required is the name of the person. Most Reiki practitioners will have a stuffed animal, such as a teddy bear, as a substitute for the person being healed to help the healer focus on the parts of the body that need healing.

I am sometimes asked if it is necessary for the person receiving the healing to know that they are receiving the healing. It is not necessary for the person to know, and indeed, sometimes the recipient is a baby or young child. It may be someone in a coma or suffering from Alzheimer's. Because of the internet and social sites like Facebook, we now have instant access to each other. This is an ideal way of asking for distant healing for someone who is critically ill.

When you send healing to a sick animal, it won't know who is sending the healing, but it will benefit from the results. I have occasionally given hands-on healing to cats and dogs, and when a cat has received enough healing, it will jump up and go away. Dogs, on the other hand, are lazy and will stay there all day. If you are required to give Reiki to a horse, always approach from the front

slowly, as they are very sensitive to Reiki.

Giving Reiki distant healing is similar to hands-on healing, but does not require as much time. Start with the intention, inviting your guardian angel, healing guides, and any past Reiki Masters to the session.

A PERSONAL STORY

I recall one Wednesday morning when I was at a Tai Chi class with my friend Angie, who is also a Reiki Master, when I suddenly felt my Reiki energy flow to Angie, who was standing next to me. When the lesson ended, Angie told me that during the class, she remembered that she had to send some healing to her brother-in-law, Mickey, who was attending a funeral at that time. Because we sometimes work together as healers, when she opened up to send healing, my energy automatically linked with hers. That evening, Angie asked her sister how the funeral had gone. Her sister said that everything went well, but that at one point, Mickey had to take his jacket off because he was too hot . . .

Also, invite the guardian angel and healing guides of the person receiving the healing. Draw the Reiki symbols in the air, repeating the mantra for each symbol three times.

The Hon-Sha-Ze-Sho-Nen symbol is the distant-healing symbol, and its translation is "no past, no present, and no future." Time and space don't exist; it is all one in the now.

Go through whatever healing session is called for given the recipient's condition. When you have finished the distant healing, give thanks to all Reiki Masters, healing guides, and guardian angels, and seal the healing with the power symbol and detach by making a cutting gesture in front of your body with both hands.

It is important to remember that sometimes things don't go the way we hoped. As healers, we must accept that there are forces higher than we are, and that we must trust and accept whatever outcomes the universe provides. Sometimes when just starting on the healing path, a person may have self-doubts because someone they are healing does not feel better or even dies. You must remember that we are only the channel for healing and cannot guarantee absolute success.

Healing the Past and the Future

Time, like distance, is an illusion. We assume that the past is behind us and the future is in front of us, and using our minds, we can travel forward and backward in this perception. There are two ways of looking at this: you can imagine the past, present, and future as three railroad tracks running parallel, which means you can cross over from one track to another because they are all happening at the same time. This might explain phenomena like déjà vu.

The second way to visualize the past and future is to imagine you are walking along a path. You can see what is directly in front of you and what is behind. Now, imagine you are also in a hot air balloon above the path; the higher you go, the farther you can see along the path behind and ahead. If there is a problem ahead, it is possible to make a detour and avoid the issue.

Most of us are familiar with the law of karma: if we exhibit a negative force in thought, word, or action, that negative energy will come back to us. On the upside, it works for positive activity as well. To receive happiness, peace, love, and friendship, we must be happy, peaceful, loving, and a true friend to all we meet. Karma shows us that how we behaved in the past can have a profound effect on us in the present moment. If we did harm to someone in a past life, we may not be aware of what we had done. Fortunately, Reiki can help heal recent and past life trauma. It is not necessary to know the details of a deed to ask for forgiveness, only that we are sincerely sorry. As the Lord's Prayer says, "forgive us our trespasses as we forgive those who trespass against us."

Healing the Past

We could dwell all day long on the evil deeds that have been done in the past and are done today, but it is better to think of the light in the world. Light will illuminate the darkest place, but when you open a box in a lit room, the darkness from the box cannot overcome the light.

Learning to let go of the past is a crucial part of healing. Imagine that you could remember every deed, both good and bad, that you did in your previous

PRESIDENTIAL FORESIGHT

It is said that President Abraham Lincoln had dreamt of his own death just before his assassination on April 14, 1865. Apparently, he shared the details of the dream with a small group of people that included his wife. In the dream, he walked into the East Room of the White House to find a corpse guarded by soldiers and surrounded by a crowd of mourners. When Lincoln asked one of the soldiers who had died, the soldier replied, "The President. He was killed by an assassin."

lives. You could not get out of bed in the morning with the weight of all those memories. Every emotional memory of anger and regret that you don't let go of is like a heavy rock that you pull around in a large sack. If you let go of this burden, you would feel happy and content, and the good news is that you *can* let go of it. There is no benefit to be had from holding on to past regrets.

When we heal the past, we face an old situation for a final time, and once we have healed it, we can let it go forever. As adults, we carry memories of times that shaped our lives. Childhood abuse or an unfaithful partner in your past can affect your relationships in the present. But it isn't good for us to go through life distrusting everyone because of the actions of one person. If, however, the situation keeps repeating itself, it may be that we are attracted to the wrong type of person because of a past trauma. Reiki can heal these situations and change our outlook for the better.

There is no blanket healing for all past deeds; we need to remove each emotional rock from the sack one at a time.

Remember it is not just the bad things that happened to us that need to be healed; we need to heal and ask for forgiveness for the wrongs we have done to others. And not all traumatic past incidents will involve interaction with other people. You may have survived a traumatic accident, such as a near-drowning or childhood illness, that happened to you and you alone or suffered the loss of a parent.

Sometimes it is hard to pinpoint the cause of the pain. The best solution is to take a pen and paper, think back to the time when you were a baby, and progress to the present day.

- How did you feel while you were growing up?
- Was there much love in the house when you were a child?
- What were your early school days like? Were you happy or were you bullied?
- Did you like your first job?
- How were your early relationships?

And so on.

When someone wants to heal the past, one strong emotion usually stands out. I gave healing to a person whose father used to beat her mother mercilessly. She was terrified of her father, and when he died she still hated him. She carried this hatred into her adult life, and it affected her health. It is not easy to get her to forgive her father, and today it is still a work in progress. Forgiving someone who has harmed us in the past is not about accepting what was done; it is just a way of ensuring that the harm we've endured does not affect our spiritual growth.

The distant-healing symbol also connects us with the past and the future. When you use this symbol, you can visualize it as a bridge to the past or the future. When working to heal the past, we need to go through the normal healing routine at the start of the healing, using all the symbols. When you are ready to start the healing, ask the recipient to focus and visualize the event in the past that needs to be healed. It is not necessary for them to share with you what happened. Draw the distant-healing symbol above them with the palm of your hand, and place the symbol into the heart of the recipient. Next,

Tip

It is also possible to send healing to your or your client's previous incarnations.

draw the mental and emotional symbol and repeat the process. While this is happening, imagine a bright white light filling the heart chakra and washing away the dark negative energy. Once you have given Reiki to the problem of the past, it will be necessary to give the recipient a full Reiki healing treatment. Sometimes it may require several sessions to remove the problem.

Healing the Future

When it comes to sending healing to the future, the process is the same as sending it into the past. I hear you asking, "How can you send healing to something that has not happened yet?" We all know that we will have to die someday, so maybe that would be the place to start. It is also a good idea to send Reiki to yourself if you need to go into the hospital for an operation. School exams, driving tests, and job interviews are other examples of the times you might need Reiki in the future. Just visualize the event and send healing energy to it.

12

REIKI AND CRYSTALS

The use of crystals in Reiki is a New Age add-on, and there is no indication that Dr. Usui used them in his healing. That does not mean that it is wrong or isn't useful, and "crystal Reiki," in which a combination of crystals and Reiki are used together, is becoming increasingly popular.

Crystals are formed in the earth over millions of years; they range from precious stones, such as diamonds, to semiprecious stones, like amethysts and quartz. Our planet is estimated to be 4.5 billion years old. It started as a swirling cloud of gas, and this contracted into a white-hot ball of molten magma. Over time (millions of years), this ball of magma cooled down to form the Earth's crust. If we compare Earth to an apple, the crust would be the skin on the apple—that is how thin it is. Molten magma still swirls inside Earth, and tectonic plates float on top of it in the lithosphere, where the magma meets the crust.

Earthquakes happen when tectonic plates shift. This can cause weaknesses in Earth's crust, which can lead to volcanoes that act like safety valves for the magma inside Earth. It is from this boiling lava that crystals are formed. As superheated, mineral-rich gases and liquids cool and harden, rocks and crystals are created. The minerals present, as well as the location and the time it takes the matter to cool, determine what type of crystals form. Crystals such as aventurine are created at high temperatures from liquid magma. Topaz, on the other hand, is formed when fluorine gases penetrate igneous rocks just as they finish cooling and solidifying. Garnets form deep in the earth when minerals melt and form crystals under intense pressure. It takes between 1 billion and 3.3 billion years for a diamond to form, and this is why they are so rare and expensive.

A History of Crystal Healing

Crystals are used to cure ailments and protect against diseases. They act as conduits for healing by allowing positive energy to flow into the body, while providing a path for negative energy outflow. Using crystals to heal is an incredibly old practice. Some of the oldest amulets found in Britain were made about thirty thousand years ago from Baltic amber; the distance the amber traveled shows how much value the people at the time placed on these amulets. Beads, bracelets, and necklaces made from lignite in the Paleolithic era (also known as the Stone Age) have been found in gravesites in Belgium and Switzerland.

The first references to crystals being used in magic formulas are from ancient Sumer. The ancient Egyptians used lapis lazuli, carnelian, turquoise, clear quartz, and emerald in their jewelry for health and protection. Lapis lazuli stones were mostly worn by women of royalty, such as Cleopatra, and dancers wore rubies in their navels to enhance their sex appeal!

In ancient China, jade was the favored healing stone and is still very popular today. Chinese medicine used crystal-tipped needles in acupuncture nearly five thousand years ago.

Choosing, Cleansing, and Storing Crystals

When it comes to choosing a crystal, there is a saying that the crystal will choose you. The best place to buy crystals is from specialist crystal shops. The people who work in them are usually very knowledgeable when it comes to the stones they sell. You can also buy crystals at mind, body, and spirit conventions, but if none of these are available to you, there is always the internet. The disadvantage of buying online is that you cannot hold the crystal before you buy to see if it resonates with you. If you do buy online, go to a website that specializes in crystals. Avoid sites that sell crystals alongside nonholistic items, such as shoes or bicycles.

Crystals are like energy batteries, and they can be cleansed and recharged when required. When you first buy a crystal, you should cleanse it because you don't know who handled it before you. The easiest way is to wash them in clean, running water. Some crystals, however, should not be washed in water. These include selenite, malachite, lapis lazuli, fluorite, calcite, desert rose, labradorite, and halite. Another way to cleanse your crystals is to pass them through the smoke of burning incense (preferably white sage). Witches tend to cleanse their crystals under the rays of the full moon or by burying them in the ground during the full moon. Putting your crystals on your windowsill on a sunny day for a few hours will also do the trick, but beware: too much sun may fade your crystals. You can also cleanse crystals by burying them each separately in sea salt for twenty-four hours, then wipe the stones carefully. (Salt is itself a crystal and has been used for centuries as a preservative and protector from negativity.) After the cleansing, the easiest way to recharge your crystals is to give them some Reiki healing.

Once you have bought your crystal and cleansed it, it is time to store it. Unpolished stones are prone to damage and chipping because of their rough edges, so if you put your crystals together in a box, make sure they don't touch each other. You can buy inexpensive little velvet pouches; these are also ideal for carrying crystals in your pocket or purse.

An old cookie tin or tackle box is also good for storing crystals, but make sure you put foam on the bottom and wrap each crystal in bubble wrap. If you have a nice selection of crystals and you want to show them off, there is a large selection of ornate glass cabinets and wooden or glass pyramids online.

Using Crystals with Reiki

To use crystals with Reiki, we need to understand the chakras and know which crystals complement and resonate with each chakra.

Root (base)	Ruby, jasper, obsidian, hematite
Sacral	Calcite, carnelian, dark topaz
Solar plexus	Tiger's eye, heliodor, yellow calcite
Heart	Rose quartz, jade
Throat	Blue tourmaline, blue topaz, blue lace agate
Third-eye	Larimar, lapis lazuli, kyanite
Crown	Amethyst, opal, quartz

MY FAVORITE CRYSTALS

To help with sleeping, I find that rose quartz works wonders. Just hold the crystal in your hand or put it under your pillow when you go to bed. Crystals are also good when meditating; I place a piece of rose quartz in each hand during meditation. Placing malachite over the third-eye chakra can be useful for spiritual guidance. Lapis lazuli is good for depression and it can be worn as a piece of jewelry. Chrysoprase encourages fidelity in personal relationships, as it promotes love.

This list of crystals and their associated chakras is just a preliminary guide; you should also use your instincts when choosing crystals for healing.

There are various ways to use the crystals during healing. For instance, you can place the appropriate crystal on each of the chakras. For the crown chakra, you can place the crystal above or on either side of the head. If a crystal moves during healing, return it to its original position. If, however, it moves again, then leave it where it is.

As a Reiki practitioner, it is your decision how much you integrate crystals into your healing routine. I normally put two bloodstone crystals on either side of a person's feet to keep them grounded during healing. I also sometimes ask people to pick one or two crystals they feel drawn to, and I place these in the palms of their hands during healing.

Crystal Wands

Crystal wands are long, narrow crystals that are cut into or naturally form a wand shape. They are normally between four and five inches long, and made from clear quartz or sometimes smoky quartz; they are pointed at one end and they may be flat or rounded at the other end. Wands are useful to Reiki

practitioners as they can be used for pinpoint healing. A wand allows a healer to focus the Reiki healing energy to the tip, with the wand acting like a powerful laser beam that reaches the area that requires the healing. The wand works on the auric field and is useful for repairing tears in the aura. When using a wand, it is important to be grounded and focused. Grounding can be done by fire agate or bloodstone at the feet of the healer.

To heal with a wand, hold the wand with the flat or rounded end close to your body. Starting at the recipient's feet, make small, circular, clockwise movements about two to six inches from the person's body. Move slowly up the body until you reach the crown chakra. The patient may experience strange sensations as negative energy is released. Imagine the wand as a laser (they always remind me of the light sabers you see in Star Wars movies). Don't wave a wand about, as you may tear someone's aura and cause damage.

Tip

Children are always attracted to crystals; however, they should only handle them under supervision. We don't want little Johnny eating your favorite crystal because he thought it was candy! And under no circumstances should you let a child handle a crystal wand.

Crystal Balls

We normally associate crystal balls with scrying, or seeing into the future, but they are also a useful means of healing. Just like with any other crystal formation, we can use a crystal ball to focus our attention on healing. Rose quartz crystal balls are ideal for healing.

If it is a small ball, hold it in your hand. If you have a large crystal ball, then put your hands on or near the ball. For self-healing, start by closing your eyes, visualizing the illness and location or a situation that needs healing. Soon you will notice the healing energy flowing from the ball. To use a crystal ball for distant healing, visualize the person you are sending the healing to as well as the illness and location that need healing.

The Reiki Crystal Grid

A Reiki crystal grid is used to send out continuous healing to those who have a long-term physical or mental illness. The best crystals for making a crystal grid are clear quartz, and a crystal wand is required to activate the grid. There are various patterns used to make a grid, but they all are circular and have a central crystal with several crystals surrounding it.

The size of a grid can be from six to twelve inches in diameter, and the outer crystals have their points facing the center, so the energy is focused on the central crystal. You can use up to twelve surrounding crystals, as long as they are all spaced evenly. Once you have your crystals arranged, put a list of names or photographs of the people who need the healing under the central crystal.

THE WONDERS OF GOLD

Although not a crystal, gold is nontoxic, is tolerated well by the body, and has antibacterial and anti-inflammatory properties. These healing powers have been recognized throughout history. Ancient Egyptians would ingest it for purification, and in ancient Rome salves made with gold were used for treating skin conditions. At banquets in Renaissance Venice, guests were served gold-covered almonds after meals to strengthen the heart, protect against rheumatism, and show off the host's wealth. Today, gold is sometimes injected into arthritic joints.

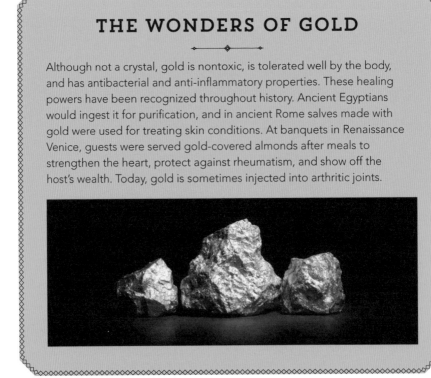

Next, use your crystal wand to draw all the Reiki symbols on to the grid. Then, to charge your Reiki grid, hold the wand in your dominant hand and imagine the energy flowing down your arm to the tip of the wand. Start by pointing the wand at the central crystal, then move the energy beam up to the outer crystal, across to the next crystal, and back down to the central crystal. Repeat this process until all the crystals have been charged. A mantra can be said while charging the crystals.

Once the crystal grid is charged, it will send out continuous healing. Grids need to be regularly charged at least once a week. The best place to keep your grid is on a flat surface, such as on a tray or a small table somewhere where it won't be disturbed.

More Power

You can increase the power of a crystal grid by using a large number of crystals, but if you do this, just use one kind of crystal because otherwise the power can become muddled. Simple crystals, such as clear quartz and amethyst are good, as you can usually find some with points or somewhat pointy sides to focus toward the center of the grid. Here are a couple of common crystal grid patterns that come from the world of sacred geometry. The first one is easy, as

all you need to do is place a crystal at the outer point of each "leaf" and then one in the center.

The next shape is more complex, as it has many circles and arcs, but you can choose to place the crystals at various points around the pattern to suit yourself. Don't forget to bring down the Reiki symbols to activate the system.

The Reiki Crystal Net

A Reiki crystal net is a larger version of a crystal grid, which is created by placing crystals around a room or even your entire home, inside and out. They

should be put into corners, on shelves, and generally tucked away where they won't get in anyone's way.

If you want to make a peaceful place outside to meditate or just to sit and be quiet once in a while. You can create a crystal net by using pebbles like the ones you pick up from the beach or a riverside. Use this sun shape as a guide for where to place the stones. You will sit inside the circle, so you can place stones on the corners of each of the triangles and all around the rim of the circle to give you the peace, protection, and rest that you need. Don't forget to imagine your Reiki symbols, especially the distant-healing symbol, to keep your crystal net energized.

A CASE HISTORY USING A REIKI CRYSTAL NET

＊ ◆ ＊

Anne had fallen down the stairs and broken a couple of small bones in her foot, and as a result a nerve had become trapped and inflamed. While it wasn't life-threatening, it was very painful and she spent most of her time confined to her easy chair, so, understandably, she was pretty fed up.

Her friend Malcolm was a Reiki healer, and when he heard about her situation, he offered to set up a Reiki net in her room.

Malcolm selected blue crystals, such as blue-lace agate, lapis lazuli, and sodalite, because these have strong healing energies and they are linked to the throat chakra. The throat chakra is linked to the planet Mercury, which is associated with the nervous system. As it happened, Anne loved all shades of blue, which would help her to resonate with the crystals in the net. Malcolm also gathered several clear quartz crystals with pointed ends.

He alternated the crystals, placing a blue one followed by a white one, and then another blue one and so on around the room, putting them into corners or placing them on shelves where they wouldn't be in anyone's way. He gave Anne a long, clear quartz crystal to hold, as this would work as an attractor for the crystal energy that would soon gather in the room.

Malcolm then took a longer clear quartz crystal wand and went around the room energizing each crystal by pointing the wand at it and then returning to Anne and her central crystal. He then sat on the floor within the net and meditated, bringing in the Reiki symbols for power, harmony, and distant healing, focusing particularly on the distant-healing symbol, as that would need to keep going after Malcolm had finished his work and left the house. He asked Dr. Usui and the Reiki Masters of the past to help him in his endeavor.

He then led Anne in a healing meditation to help the process along. Here is the meditation that he used.

REIKI HEALING MEDITATION

- Close your eyes and relax.

- Breathe evenly. Focus on your breathing.

- Imagine yourself floating in a warm sea with a palm-fringed beach nearby.

- While you are floating around, imagine light coming down from the universe.

- The light is mainly white but it contains flecks of pale blue.

- You feel relaxed and happy.

- Now imagine a powerful beam of light focusing on your bad foot.

- It surrounds the foot and pours into it, through it, and swirls around it, cooling and calming the swollen nerves and mending the broken bones and ligaments.

- Now slowly and gently go to the shore. Leave that world behind as you come back to this room once again.

- Open your eyes and look around.

Malcolm now told Anne to tuck her central crystal down beside the cushion of her chair on the same side as her bad foot. He also handed Anne a glass of water to sip. He then spent the next hour giving her a full Reiki healing, while she remained seated in her easy chair.

A few days later, Malcolm reenergized the net by sitting quietly in his own home and focusing his mind on Anne and the net and sending it the distant-healing symbol. He did this again a few days after that.

THE OUTCOME

It would be nice to say that Anne experienced an instant miracle cure after the net-setting session, but that wasn't quite the case, although she definitely felt more relaxed than before. The following day, Anne did notice that she was in less pain, and she was soon able to stop taking the strong pain killers that she had been on and substitute them for over-the-counter medicine. She improved as the days went by, and she was soon able to hobble into the kitchen to cook meals.

When she went back to the hospital for an X-ray and a checkup on the foot, the doctor was astonished at the speedy way in which the swollen and inflamed nerve was settling down, and the rate of healing in the small bones of her foot. Anne told him about the Reiki net and watched the doctor shake his head in amazement. The doctor then said, "If it did the trick, Anne, it was worth it, but I can't say that I understand how it worked."

Well Anne didn't understand it either, but she was very glad that it had worked.

13

AURA CLEARING AND SHAMANIC HEALING

Before an illness manifests in the physical body, it manifests as a negative psychic energy in the auras. These negative psychic energies can be detected by scanning the body with the nondominant hand or pendulum. When someone is very ill or is in danger of becoming so, Reiki healers can perform what's known as an *aura clearing*. Also known as *psychic surgery*, it is taught at the Advanced Reiki Training (ART) level. In all my years as a Reiki practitioner, apart from my training course, I have had to carry out only one Aura Clearing. I believe that, because it is so powerful, it should be used only when everything else has failed.

Aura clearing can mean many things. To some it refers to drawing negative energy out of the energy field or body; to others it means the removal of harmful thought forms that have their roots in the past. It was not part of the original Reiki teaching but instead came about as Reiki progressed in the New Age movement. Aura clearing is totally noninvasive and safe when done by an accredited Reiki practitioner, and it is possible to do aura clearing on oneself.

Aura Clearing

Psychic surgery is now more commonly called aura clearing. This may be due to the bad press around certain practices in the Philippines and South America in which "healers" were faking incisions by running a finger along the patient's body, apparently going through the skin without using any surgical instruments and pretending to pull out "tumors." Using sleight-of-hand, the frauds were actually squeezing animal blood and chicken hearts and livers from a hand-held balloon onto their patients. This type of fake psychic surgery is big business around the world, especially in Manila, where there are several hundred practicing psychic surgeons. Many of them work out of hotels and charge large fees for their services.

On the other side of psychic surgery, there are some good, sincere healers. They mostly come from a spiritual church background where there is a sincere desire to heal. This kind of spiritual healer performs noninvasive psychic surgery and trance healing. With trance healing, the energies come directly from spirit. With the spiritual beings so much closer, this form of healing can work at a deep level on emotional and spiritual issues.

As we have already said, people get ill when they have blockages in their energy flow. These blockages can be ideas or emotions that have a negative effect on our well-being. They may originate from early-childhood abuse, current traumas, or even past-life events. If a blockage is left to fester, it can affect the body's organs. In extreme cases when regular Reiki treatments aren't having an effect, an aura clearing may be necessary. This takes about two hours, as it needs to be followed by a complete Reiki session.

Tip

If a person has major physical or psychological problems, it is your duty to recommend that he or she seek a licensed health care provider, and to let the person know that the purpose of Reiki healing is to work in conjunction with regular medical care, and not to replace it.

The Procedure

The first step is to find out what the problem is and to give it an identity. This allows the healer and the recipient to focus on the cause and deal with it. It is not necessary for the healer to know the specifics of the cause—it might be something the person does not wish to discuss, and as Reiki practitioners, we are not qualified psychologists. As long as the person is aware of the problem that needs to be healed, that is fine.

The next steps are to give the issue some form and to find where in the body the problem is located. You will find that in the majority of cases, the problem will be close to one of the major organs in the body. Start by asking the client to close his eyes and meditate on the issue. It doesn't matter if the client is sitting or lying down during the healing process.

Ask: "If the cause of this problem were to exist in a part of your body, which part would it be in?" This way, you will be able to locate the specific chakra that is being affected. Interestingly, the client will normally know where it is in the body. Most problems link to the lower chakras, but if the client is in mourning, it will be affecting the heart chakra.

Once you have a location for the issue, you need to give it substance. You can do this by asking questions, such as:

- What color is it?
- How big is it?
- How heavy is it?
- What shape is it? Square, round, pyramid shaped, spiky?
- What is the texture of the surface? Smooth, rough, bubbly, soft, or hard?
- Is it warm or cold?

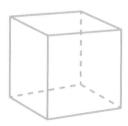 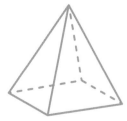 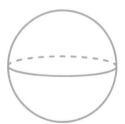

By asking the client to describe the problem in a visual form, it makes it easier for the client to monitor the change after the healing.

Ask the client if he is willing to let go of this problem completely and to be healed, and then tell him that you are going send the problem up to God or the higher power. Tell him to focus on the shape of the problem and to be willing to let it go.

What comes next is a complex ritual that will remove the issue that is causing the problem, but this knowledge is only available to those who are Reiki Masters or who have had received Advanced Reiki Training (ART).

When an aura healing is complete, the client should be aware of the change in the shape, size, and weight of the issue that caused the problem. Depending on the severity of the problem, more than one session may be needed.

Shamanic Healing

Shamanic healing is one of the oldest healing practices, stretching back thousands of years and linking indigenous cultures across the globe. A major aspect of the shamanic way of life is "journeying" through three realms that are quite different from each other. They all have distinct qualities and different inhabitants. There is the upper world, which may be thought of as heaven though people from different cultures experience different imagery. Christians might experience saints, angels, or Jesus, while a Hindu might experience Lord Shiva or Ganesh. The upper world is a place of wisdom, love, healing, and compassion. By contrast, the lower world is the realm of Mother Earth. Here there are Human People, Animal People, Standing

People (trees), and Plant People, all of whom can provide us with wisdom and healing gifts. In the middle world, we come close to what Christians would call hell; there is pain and disease, poverty, inequality, plagues, wars, and famine. Journeying to these different worlds is initially done under the supervision of an experienced shamanic practitioner and then eventually on one's own.

Shamanic healing is an energy-based therapy, and health issues are seen as being connected to loss of energy or power. Healers called *medicine men* or *shaman*s work to balance these issues. They can communicate with spirits and "journey" to spirit realms with the help of their own spirit guides. Sometimes they bring back advice for their patients. During a healing session, a shaman may use drums, rattles, chimes, chanting, and song as well as "sacred smudge"—a method of burning herbs and incense to spiritually cleanse and bless the area.

Shamanic healers also do a "soul retrieval" ritual when a person feels or thinks something is missing or feels empty inside and does not know how to get back to normality. Soul loss may be caused by an event in the present life or carried over from a past life. Soul retrieval is a process of returning the lost energy, the essence of you are and what is yours, back to you. A soul retrieval ceremony is complicated, often taking multiple sessions, but it brings positive change to a person mentally, emotionally, and physically.

❋ ❋ ❋

14

YOUR OWN
REIKI PRACTICE

If you decide to offer Reiki to the public, the easiest way to start a practice is to work from home. There are advantages and disadvantages to this. On the plus side, you don't have to pay rent for an office or pay commuting costs. (If you live in a rental apartment, you should check your lease before you start.) You also have flexibility with the hours you work. For instance, some clients will have day jobs and will be available only in the evening. However, there are some things you should take into account:

- Will having a Reiki practice at home disrupt your family life?
- How does your partner feel about part of the home being used for healing?
- If you have small children, can you guarantee that you won't be disturbed?
- It is the same with pets.
- Decide what hours you are available for healing sessions based on when you have the most peace and quiet.
- Make a designated area for your practice that is used only for healing. Do not be tempted to let other members of the family use it just because it is a nice, quiet place to do homework or for playing games.
- At most, the only electrical items that should be in the room are a lamp and a CD player to play healing music.
- The room should be well ventilated and warm but not hot. The décor should be neutral. Avoid too much clutter because negative energy loves to attach to clutter.
- You may want to light a white candle but not a scented one, because scents can have an effect on some people.
- You may wish to play music that is specially composed for Reiki healing, with each track lasting five minutes, so you know when to move on to the next hand position.
- Parking and transportation for clients is also worth thinking about. Are there plenty of places to park nearby? Are you on a regular bus or subway route?
- Nobody wants to receive healing from someone with bad breath or body odor. Strong perfume or aftershave should also be avoided.
- Use all the means you can to market your skills, such as business cards and leaflets, working at psychic fairs, posting flyers in local shops and on bulletin boards, giving free sessions at charity events, and so on.

Before a client arrives, I spend some time in a quiet, relaxed state, and I invite my guardian angel and healing guides to be present for the healing. If I have not already done so, I will put the Reiki symbols around the room. When the client arrives, I normally have a little chat about how they are feeling and if they have any specific issues they want me to address. There is no need to be too hung up on these things, because the Reiki will go where it is needed. It is not unusual for people to come to have healing on their back only to find the problem is somewhere else.

If it is the client's first visit, you will need to create a record for them, and you have a duty to respect the client's confidentiality, so all personal information needs to be kept confidential and all records kept in a secure, locked place. All records should be kept for at least seven years and shredded when no longer required.

A Client Record Form

- Date
- Client's Name
- Address
- Phone number
- Email
- An emergency contact name and number, and the contact's relationship to the client
- Client's current medication and dosage
- Client's doctor's name and address
- Has the client had Reiki before?
- Brief description of why the client wants Reiki healing

Reiki Treatment Disclaimer

In addition to the client's record, it will be necessary to have a disclaimer for the client to read, date, and sign. Here is an example of a disclaimer form:

> Healing and medicine are two separate disciplines. Reiki is the art of healing, not the practice of medicine. Reiki is intended to be a supplement to—but not a substitute for—professional medical care and treatment. In the case of any serious medical ailment or condition, you should always consult your doctor for advice.
>
> Reiki practitioners never diagnose conditions; perform medical treatments; make any medical claims; prescribe therapies, remedies, or medication; or interfere with any form of treatment prescribed by a licensed medical professional. I will endeavor to do my very best to help you, but I cannot offer any guarantee of success.
>
> As the client, you will always be treated with the utmost respect and integrity. Confidentiality is an underpinning principle of Reiki, and you can be sure that all personal data and information will be kept safe, complete, and private at all times, both during treatment and for a minimum of seven years afterward.

The client signs the document to show he or she understands and accepts all of its terms and conditions, and is willing to proceed with the treatment.

Once your client has settled down, it is a good idea to offer a drink of water. After the initial pleasantries, you can explain exactly what Reiki is, that the treatment is nonintrusive, and that there is no need to remove any clothing except shoes and glasses, if worn. Once the client is lying on the therapy bed, it is a good idea to cover him with a blanket to keep him warm. It is not unusual for the client to fall asleep during the healing.

With the room dim and the healing music playing, start by asking the client to close his eyes, take a few deep breaths, and clear his mind of any thoughts. I tell him to listen to the music, as this helps clear the mind. Explain that nothing will happen for a few minutes while you blend with his energy and state your intentions for the healing to take place.

After the first couple of sessions with a client, they will know what to expect, so you can allot less time for their visit.

READING PEOPLE'S POSTURE

When people hunch their shoulders, they are showing signs of stress, but if they lean forward, this may be a sign of anger. People may also have a closed posture in which they try to obscure a part of their body that has experienced trauma. They may try to protect themselves by crossing their legs or placing their hands across the stomach. A woman may put her purse on her lap to protect her base or sacral chakra, or she may move her hands to her throat when talking. A slouch posture suggests fatigue. Relaxed hands indicate confidence and self-assurance, while clenched hands are a sign of stress or anger.

Payment

When it comes to charging for a Reiki healing, there are conflicting views. Some believe that because we receive the healing energy from the universe, we should give it free, while others think that if Reiki is given freely, those receiving the healing won't appreciate it. In fact, Dr. Usui and Mrs. Takata believed that when you give healing energy, the practitioner must be honored for his or her time and services. Furthermore, if Reiki is your only occupation, you will need an income from your work in order to survive.

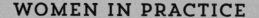

WOMEN IN PRACTICE

If you work at home, allow male clients into your home only when your family is around. If you use premises other than your home, do your work when other people are around, and deal with men only if you have people within earshot who will come to your aid if needed. Don't advertise in papers or magazines. Instead, market your services at mind, body, and spirit festivals and by word of mouth.

Professionals who work in the MBS fields have spent a lot of time and effort, and often a considerable amount of money, on training. Practitioners also lay out money for their consulting room, therapy bed, business equipment, and other accoutrements, so in my view, payment is a fair and necessary part of providing Reiki healing to the public. The best way for you to gauge how much to charge for a healing session is to see what other healers in your area charge.

✻ ✻ ✻

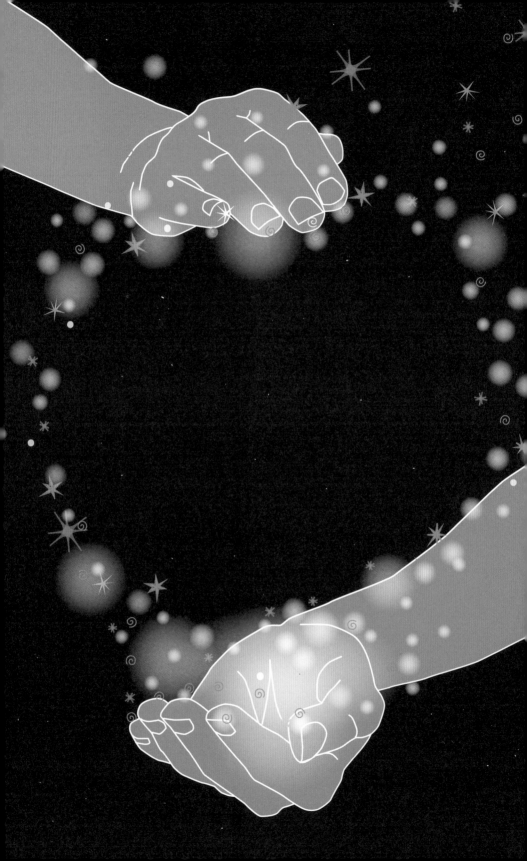

CONCLUSION

There is no doubt that Reiki is a form of spiritual as well as energy healing, and it seems that Reiki is moving in two directions. One direction is for Reiki practitioners who like to embrace all the methods of New Age healing, such as crystals, angels, rainbow Reiki, and White Dove Reiki. The other is for those who practice a spiritual kind of Reiki, where there is emphasis on how the practitioner lives, strictly adhering to and living by the Reiki principles, as in Holy Fire Reiki and Karuna Reiki. Healing starts in the mind, and if you are drawn toward crystal Reiki or Holy Fire Reiki, it will work, because it is all from the same divine source.

As you saw at the start of this book, I knew nothing about Reiki or energy healing until my wife fell ill. This hardship led me down an unexpected road and has given me a life that is more interesting and more meaningful than my years of retirement might otherwise have been. Remember that Reiki is a spiritual journey, and you may be surprised where it takes you.

I wish you good luck on your own Reiki journey.

❁ ❁ ❁

ABOUT THE AUTHOR

Des Hynes had a long career in the British Royal Navy, traveling the world and observing a variety of beliefs and lifestyles, but it was when his much-loved wife, Viv, battled with cancer that he saw how Reiki healing helped her to cope with the treatment. This experience encouraged Des to train as a Reiki healer, eventually becoming an Usui Holy Fire Reiki Master/Teacher.

He then went on to take an interest in energy healing as a whole, and to look into the way the mind and body work together. He believes that the mind has a large part to play in matters related to health, but he absolutely believes that electronic equipment, powerlines and towers, and so on also contribute to some modern illnesses.

IMAGE CREDITS

INDEX